D0368773

SCHOOL LAW CASEBOOK SERIES — No. 4

The Law
Governing Pupils

By
LEE O. GARBER
and
NEWTON EDWARDS

The Interstate
Printers and Publishers
Danville, Illinois

Library of Congress
Catalog Card Number: 62-20681

CONTENTS

INTRODUCTION

With the publication of this casebook, the first cycle is completed. The four casebooks now available provide complete coverage for the first semester of a course in "School Law." The three preceding books deal with "The Public School in Our Governmental Structure," "The Law Relating to the Creation, Alteration, and Dissolution of School Districts," and "The Law Governing Teaching Personnel." Casebooks planned for the second cycle will cover the law as it relates to school officers; liability of school districts, officers, and employees; school buildings; and school finance. Work on these has already begun and their publication will follow shortly. When these are completed, casebooks covering the entire field of school law will be available. These books will be welcomed by those professors of school law who are seeking supplementary and illustrative materials and by those desirous of using the case method of instruction. Likewise, they will be welcomed by professors of other subjects who have sought material of this sort to be used in integrating school law with their specialties.

The authors speak authoritatively. They need no introduction, as they have established themselves and are recognized as specialists in the field of "School Law." Newton Edwards, Professor Emeritus, University of Chicago, has written numerous articles dealing with this subject and is the author of the well-known leading text in this field—*The Courts and the Public Schools*. Lee O. Garber, Professor of Education, University of Pennsylvania, has prepared the *Yearbook of School Law* annually since 1950. In addition, he is known for his articles of timely interest which have been regular features of *The Nation's Schools* for the past decade.

Russell L. Guin
Publisher

Authors' Preface

This casebook follows the same pattern as the three that preceded it. It contains one section dealing with "Legal Principles" and one with "Court Decisions." The decisions in the second section have been selected to illustrate the basic principles mentioned in the first. The four books, taken together, give a coverage of the material generally included in the first semester of a course in "School Law"—a course for teachers and administrators, alike.

In addition to finding its place in courses in "School Law," it is hoped that this book will prove of value in supplementing the material offered in such courses as those entitled "Law and the Teacher," "Law and the Pupil," and "The Administration of Pupil Personnel." Likewise, it is also hoped that this book will find a place in undergraduate teacher-education courses designed to give the students a concept of the rights, duties, and obligations of teachers and pupils alike.

Again the authors wish to state that the legal principles are not exhaustive. Those included were, however, carefully selected on the basis of their importance as well as their uniform acceptance. Because the courts in all jurisdictions do not, and should not necessarily, agree in all their holdings, exceptions may be found to many principles. To mention all deviations from principles would be impossible and inadvisable in a treatment of this sort. Students must be aware of this limitation and should attempt to identify those exceptions, if any, recognized by the courts in their particular states.

Lee O. Garber
Newton Edwards

I.

LEGAL PRINCIPLES

The Law Governing Pupils

Authority of the State to Require Attendance

Education is so essential to the general welfare in the democratic state that the state may require children to attend a public, private, or parochial school. A statute requiring children to attend a public school, however, is violative of the due-process-of-law clause of the Fourteenth Amendment. A compulsory-education law must be reasonably administered; parents can always set up the defense that they had good reason for not sending a child to school. A compulsory-attendance law cannot be enforced against a married girl of school age. While courts are in disagreement, according to the weight of authority parents may teach their own children at home or employ a tutor to teach them, but, in order to meet the compulsory-attendance law's requirements, they must be able to show that the children are receiving substantially the same educational opportunity they would have received in the public schools. But some courts hold that if the statue requires that the child attend a public or private school, education by the parent is not the equivalent of attendance at a private school. As a rule, parents will not be permitted to set up the defense that the law is in violation of their religious principles.

Residence of Pupils and the Right to Attend School

In interpreting statutes governing the right of pupils to attend a particular school, the courts agree that the domicile of the child is the domicile of the parents, or of the last surviving parent. A number of the older court decisions have held that a child must have a legal domicile in a school district in order to attend its schools free of tuition; pupils who were separated from their parents and lived in a school district in which they did not have a legal domicile were denied the right to attend school free of tuition. The more recent and the better-reasoned decisions hold that a child does not have to have a legal domicile in a district in order to attend its schools free of charge; it is sufficient if he is actually residing in the district for some other reason than to take advantage of its educational opportunities. Where parents are living in a school district temporarily for some purpose other than to take advantage of the public schools of the district, they are commonly held to have the right to send their children to school free of charge. But where parents are residing temporarily in a district in order to take advantage of its schools, they are required to pay tuition. The fact that a parent owns property and pays taxes in a district in which he does not reside does not entitle him to send his children to the schools of that district free of tuition.

Statutes frequently provide that, under certain conditions, pupils may attend school in districts in which they are nonresidents; in such cases the statute must be strictly complied with because the right of attendance is purely statutory. And in most instances, though not in all, it has been held that statutes of this kind violate the principles of uniformity of taxation, unless they provide that the home district of the pupil shall pay its proportionate share of the cost of school maintenance in the district to which the pupil is transferred. Pupils living in territory under the exclusive jurisdiction of the United States government are not entitled to attend the schools of the community free of tuition.

Racial Discrimination and Segregation

The Supreme Court of the United States has ruled that to deny a pupil the right to attend the public school of his choice because of race or color violates the equal-protection-of-the-law clause of the Fourteenth Amendment. The court directed that the educational authorities in the states proceed to eliminate racial discrimination in the public schools "with all deliberate speed." During recent years a number of federal district and circuit courts, in interpreting and applying the Supreme Court decisions, have described the type of organization required to satisfy the criteria implicit in these decisions. These lower federal courts have held that the Supreme Court decisions do not require integration but merely forbid the use of governmental force to enforce segregation. The Supreme Court decisions, it is said, do not compel the mixing of the races or the reshuffling of the pupils in any school system. What these decisions do require is that all pupils, regardless of race or color, have free access, if they so desire it, to the schools maintained by state authority. The federal courts have also ruled that the transition from a discriminatory school system to a non-discriminatory system need not necessarily be abrupt; the transition may be gradual, but it must be made "with all deliberate speed."

Pupils who complain that they have been denied their constitutional right to attend public school may take their case directly to a federal court without resort to the state courts. It is a generally accepted principle of law, however, that where the statutes provide administrative remedies these must be exhausted before the courts will assume jurisdiction. If the remedies on their face are inadequate, the courts will assume jurisdiction without their having been exhausted. It has been held that where the remedy provided for in the statute is a resort to the courts, the remedy is judicial and not administrative, and it need not be exhausted before resort can be had to the courts.

A number of states have enacted "Pupil Assignment Statutes" in which they set up the criteria for assigning pupils to particular schools. Where these criteria are reasonable and not based on race or color, the courts hold the statutes constitutional on their face. But a statute, because of its "facial constitutionality," cannot be made to serve as an instrument for maintaining or effecting a system of racial segregation. The same general principles apply to the placement plans of local school boards.

Board Regulations Governing Attendance

School attendance is a privilege extended by the state and not an absolute right; the courts, therefore, will sustain the authority of school boards to reject applicants for admission who do not conform to the reasonable requirements established by the board. School boards have the authority to classify pupils on the basis of scholarship. It has been held that pupils who are physically or mentally defective to the point that their presence would be harmful to other pupils may be excluded from the public schools.

Transportation of Pupils

Statutes authorizing local school boards to provide transportation of pupils to and from school have uniformly been held to be constitutional. Some courts have held that local school boards do not have the authority to spend public funds to provide transportation unless authorized to do so by statute; other courts have held that school boards have the implied authority to provide transportation. The courts will sustain the discretion of a school board in establishing and maintaining transportation routes and in determining what pupils will be transported, unless the board acts unreasonably and abuses its discretion. The courts will not require that conveyances be sent to the home of each child or that transportation be provided for children living in isolated or inaccessible places. In providing transportation for pupils, a board of education must treat all who are in the same class or category alike.

School districts are not, as a rule, liable for injuries to pupils sustained while being transported to and from school, in the absence of a statute to the contrary. The principle of nonliability in the performance of a governmental function does not, however apply to a bus driver. A bus driver will be held personally liable for injuries to pupils growing out of his own negligence. A bus driver will be held to be negligent unless he exercised the degree of care any reasonably prudent person would have exercised. And this reasonably prudent care must be exercised in all his relations to pupils while being transported—condition of the bus, speed at which it is driven, the discipline of pupils while on the bus, and the circumstances under which pupils are permitted to board or leave the bus. Whether a bus driver exercised due care in any particular case is a matter to be determined by the jury. And the verdict of the jury will stand unless it is against the manifest weight of authority or contrary to law. It has been held that, since a school board is not liable for injuries to pupils while being transported, it does not have the implied authority to carry insurance to protect itself against the negligence of its employees. Statutory authority to carry insurance does not affect the governmental immunity of a school board, and in no case will a board be held for damages in an amount greater than that provided for in the insurance policy. The _ultra vires_ act of a school board in carrying liability insurance will not necessarily excuse an insurance company from paying the amount stipulated in its insurance contract, so it has been held.

Rules and Regulations of School Boards Affecting Pupils

It is well established by many court decisions that school boards have the authority to make and enforce any reasonable rules governing the conduct of pupils. The reasonableness of a board rule will be determined by the facts in each particular case. In determining the reasonableness of a rule, a court will not substitute its own discretion for that of the board; the enforcement of the rule will not be enjoined unless the rule is clearly unreasonable. A board may not, however, enforce a rule with respect to a matter outside its jurisdiction.

A board may enforce any reasonable rule with respect to the time and age at which beginning pupils may enter school. Rules regulating the dress of pupils have been held to be reasonable. A board may make the taking of a physical examination a condition of school attendance, and it may exclude from school pupils whose presence would jeopardize the health of other pupils. Statutes which authorize or require vaccination against smallpox or immunization against diphtheria as a prerequisite of school attendance have been held to be constitutional, as have also school-board regulations to this effect adopted under permissive statutes. In the absence of statutory authority, as a general rule, the courts will not enforce a rule requiring vaccination against smallpox as a condition of school attendance unless there is an actual or threatened epidemic of smallpox in the community. A pupil cannot defeat the operation of a rule or law requiring vaccination on the ground that it violates his freedom of conscience. (A board of health, like a board of education, does not have the implied authority to exclude children from school unless they have been vaccinated, in the absence of an actual or threatened epidemic of smallpox in the community.)

Statutes authorizing or requiring boards of education to expel pupils who belong to fraternities or secret societies have been held to be constitutional in a number of jurisdictions. Boards of education have the implied authority to limit the privileges of pupils who maintain membership in fraternities or secret societies. It has been held, too, that boards of education may deny to married pupils the right to participate in such extracurricular activities as football.

The state has the authority to require the pupils in its schools to take those studies that are essential for good citizenship. In the absence of statute authorizing a board of education to require that pupils pursue a particular subject, according to the weight of authority, a parent may make any reasonable selection of the studies his child will pursue from those offered by the school. A school board has the right to prescribe the method of instruction in any particular subject.

It is well established that a school board may enforce its reasonable rules and regulations governing the conduct of pupils off the school grounds and after school hours. A board of education may discipline a pupil for misbehavior wherever committed, provided it directly affects school discipline and is calculated to impair the efficiency of the school.

Bible Reading and Religious Instruction

Many states have constitutional provisions prohibiting sectarian instruction in the public schools or the use of public funds for the support of religious or sectarian schools. In some states the courts have held that Bible reading is sectarian instruction and violative of state constitutional provisions prohibiting instruction of this kind. Most state courts, however, have ruled that statutes or board regulations permitting the reading of the Bible, the saying of The Lord's Prayer, or the singing of hymns are not in violation of prohibitions against religious or sectarian instruction. So far the Supreme Court of the United States has not had occasion to decide whether Bible reading in the public school is violative of the federal constitution. A United States District Court, however, has held that compulsory Bible reading is violative of the First Amendment. A board rule that permits religious instructors to come into a public-school building to give sectarian instruction to pupils whose parents desire it violates the federal constitution. A school board may, however, permit pupils to be released from school time to attend sectarian instruction at some other place in the community. It is not violative of the federal constitution for a school board to pay the cost of the transportation of pupils to a parochial school.

Discipline and Punishment of Pupils

The right to attend public school is not absolute; a board of education may expel from school any pupil who disobeys any reasonable rule of the board. Likewise, a pupil may be expelled for general misconduct that does not violate any specific rule of the board. In the nature of his duties, a teacher has the right to exclude a pupil from school until the matter has been passed upon by the school board. Unless the statute requires it, it is not necessary to give the pupil notice of his suspension or a hearing before excluding him from school. A board of education does not have authority to expel a pupil from school for an indefinite period; the general rule is that expulsion does not extend beyond the current school year. Where a board is seeking to enforce an unreasonable rule, the remedy of the pupil is to secure an injunction against its enforcement. If a pupil has been illegally excluded from school he may obtain a writ of mandamus to enforce his reinstatement.

Under the common law the teacher stands in *loco parentis* in respect to the corporal punishment of his pupils. He may, therefore, administer any reasonable corporal punishment for offenses within the jurisdiction of the board of education, and the jurisdiction of the board, as has been stated, extends to acts committed off the school grounds if they directly affect the discipline and good order of the school. According to one line of decision, the teacher will not be held for damages in the discipline of pupils by corporal punishment if he acts without malice, and inflicts no lasting or permanent injury upon the pupil. In determining whether the punishment is reasonable or not, courts generally hold that it should be adapted to the nature of the offense and the age, sex, and size of the pupil. The courts commonly give the teacher the benefit of the doubt, and it must be shown that the punishment was clearly excessive and unreasonable before the teacher will be held liable.

II.

COURT DECISIONS

COURT DECISIONS

1. *"Education is so essential to the general welfare . . . that the state may require children to attend a public, private, or parochial school"* (p. 3).

STATE V. JACKSON,
71 N.H. 552, 53 A. 1021 (1902)
(Decided by the Supreme Court of New Hampshire)

[When Samuel Jackson was convicted of violation of the school law for failure to have his daughter enrolled in public or private school, he excepted. A higher court sustained his exception. He contended, first, that the compulsory education act was unconstitutional. He also contended that his daughter, ten years of age, had not been enrolled in school because she was in feeble health and that he took her from school believing, in good faith, that her attendance thereat would seriously injure her. In its decision the court first held the act was constitutional, but it also agreed that if it was necessary for the parent to withdraw his child from school for her own physical well-being he had that right without first obtaining an excuse.]

REMICK, J. The motion to quash the complaint on the ground that the statute upon which it was founded is unconstitutional was properly denied. The statute is as follows: "Every person having the custody and control of a child between the ages of eight and fourteen years, residing in a school district in which a public school is annually taught, shall cause such child to attend the public school all the time such school is in session, unless the child shall be excused by the school board of the district because his physical or mental condition is such as to prevent his attendance for the period required, or because he was instructed in the English language in a private school approved by the school board, for a number of weeks equal to that in which the public school was in session, in the common English branches, or, having acquired those branches, in other more advanced studies. Any person who does not comply with the requirements of this section shall be fined ten dollars for the first offense and twenty dollars for every subsequent offense." Pub. St. c. 93, § 14; Laws 1901, c. 61, § 1. That education of the citizen is essential to the stability of the state, is a proprosition too plain for discussion. As a mere generalization of our own, it would command immediate and universal assent. . . .

•   •   •   •   •   •   •   •   •   •   •   •   •   •   •

. . . For the diffusion of knowledge and learning through the community the legislature have the undoubted right, as against the mere will and pleasure of the parent, to require him to send his child to school; but they cannot repeal the natural, common-law, and constitutional right of the parent "to do whatever apparently is reasonably necessary to be done in defense" of the life of his child. . . . So, if apparently reasonably necessary for a parent to keep or withdraw his child from school, in defense of the child's life, without first applying for excuse by the school board, the legislature cannot compel him to first make such application.

Guides for Class Discussion

1. Compare this case with *Pierce* v. *Society of Sisters, infra.*
2. Compare this case with *State* v. *Superior Court, infra.*
3. Compare this case with *Bissell* v. *Davison, infra.*
4. What is the logic back of the legal principle illustrated by this case?

2. *"A statute requiring children to attend a public school . . . is violative of the due-process-of-law clause of the Fourteenth Amendment"* (p. 3).

PIERCE v. SOCIETY OF SISTERS,
268 U. S. 510 (1925)
(Decided by the Supreme Court of the United States)

[In Oregon the legislature passed a law requiring all parents of children between the ages of eight and sixteen to enroll them in public schools. The constitutionality of this law was questioned when two private schools brought actions to restrain its enforcement. They contended that the law interfered, unreasonably, with the liberty of parents to direct the education of their children and that it also interfered with the right of the private schools to enjoy the use of their property and was, therefore, violative of the Fourteenth Amendment.]

Mr. Justice McReynolds delivered the opinion of the Court.

. . . .

The challenged Act, effective September 1, 1926, requires every parent, guardian or other person having control or charge or custody of a child between eight and sixteen years to send him "to a public school for the period of time a public school shall be held during the current year" in the district where the child resides; and failure so to do is declared a misdemeanor. . . . The manifest purpose is to compel general attendance at public schools by normal children, between eight and sixteen, who have not completed the eighth grade. And without doubt enforcement of the statute would seriously impair, perhaps destroy, the profitable features of appellees' business and greatly diminish the value of their property.

. . . .

Under the doctrine of *Meyer* v. *Nebraska*, 262 U. S. 390, we think it entirely plain that the Act of 1922 unreasonably interferes with the liberty of parents and guardians to direct the upbringing and education of children under their control. As often heretofore pointed out, rights guaranteed by the Constitution may not be abridged by legislation which has no reasonable relation to some purpose within the competency of the State. The fundamental theory of liberty upon which all governments in this Union repose excludes any general power of the State to standardize its children by forcing them to accept instruction from public teachers only. The child is not the mere creature of the State; those who nurture him and direct his destiny have the right, coupled with the high duty, to recognize and prepare him for additional obligation.

Appellees are corporations and therefore, it is said, they cannot claim for themselves the liberty which the Fourteenth Amendment guarantees. Accepted in the proper sense, this is true. . . . But they have business and property for which they claim protection. These are threatened with destruction through the unwarranted compulsion which appellants are exercising over present and prospective patrons of their schools. And this court has gone very far to protect against loss threatened by such actions.

. . . .

Generally is it entirely true, as urged by counsel, that no person in any business has such an interest in possible customers as to enable him to restrain exercise of proper power of the State upon the ground that he will be deprived of patronage. But the injunctions here sought are not against the exercise of any *proper* power. Plaintiffs asked protection against arbitrary, unreasonable and unlawful interference with their patrons and the consequent destruction of their business and property. Their interest is clear and immediate. . . .

. . . .

The decrees below are

Affirmed.

Guides for Class Discussion

1. Explain the court's reasoning.
2. Do you think the question of property rights influenced the court's thinking unduly?
3. How far does this decision go in limiting the authority of the state in educational affairs?
4. What are the implications of this decision with respect to the state's authority to enact laws controlling private and parochial schools?

3. "A compulsory-attendance law cannot be enforced against a married girl of school age" (p. 3).

In re State In Interest of Goodwin,
214 La. 1062, 39 So. (2d) 731 (1949)
(Decided by the Supreme Court of Louisiana)

[In this case a girl 14 years of age was taken into custody by juvenile officers on charges of being a juvenile delinquent "by being truant from school." The court released her in custody of a friend who promised to return her to the detention home after attendance at church. That afternoon she was married. The marriage license gave her age as 16, and her mother had given her consent. She and her husband lived together as man and wife before she returned to the detention home. Two days later, proceedings were instituted for her release. The lower court found she was not a delinquent on account of truancy but that she was a neglected child.]

FOURNET, Justice.

. . . .

While this marriage was consummated in violation of Article 92 of the Revised Civil Code as amended, by Act No. 140 of 1934, which prohibits ministers and magistrates from marrying any female under the age of 16, and also in violation of Article 99, as amended by Act No. 312 of 1948, which fixes a waiting period of 72 hours after the issuance of the license during which such ministers and magistrates are prohibited from performing a marriage, there being no other impediment to the marriage, it is, nevertheless, a valid marriage under the jurisprudence of this state. . . . The redactors of our code and the legislature in amending these articles did not provide for the nullity of the marriages performed in violation thereof, but, instead, provided in the former case for the removal from office of the magistrate performing a ceremony in violation thereof and for the suspension forever of the minister's right to perform such ceremonies, and, in the latter case, for the revocation of the right to perform a marriage for one year. Consequently, Clydell is irrevocably emancipated by this marriage as a matter of right . . . and although until she reaches the age of 18 she is not relieved of all of the disabilities that attach to minority by this emancipation, she is relieved of parental control and . . . is no longer amenable to the compulsory school attendance law of this state. Furthermore, having acquired the status of a wife, it is not only her right but also her duty to live with her husband at their matrimonial domicile and to follow him wherever he chooses to reside. . . .

. . . .

While we view with sympathy the trial judge's deep convictions of the tragedy inherent in the marriage of girls of tender years and his skepticism of any ultimate good resulting therefrom, we recognize the basic fact that under our system of government the matter of fixing the public policy of this state with respect to the age at which people may or may not marry as well as fixing the status of marriages solemnized in violation thereof lies exclusively within the province of the legislative branch.

Guides for Class Discussion

1. Do you think that the rule that "marriage emancipates a minor female" is equitable? Give reasons.
2. Would a statute requiring married females of school age to continue in attendance at school be constitutional?
3. Do you think the courts would also hold that marriage emancipates a minor male as far as school attendance is concerned?

4. "While courts are in disagreement, according to the weight of authority parents may teach their own children at home or employ a tutor to teach them, but, in order to meet the compulsory-attendance law's requirements, they must be able to show that the children are receiving substantially the same educational opportunity they would have received in the public schools. But some courts hold that if the statute requires that the child attend a public or private school, education by the parent is not the equivalent of attendance at a private school" (p. 3).

STATE v. SUPERIOR COURT,

55 Wash. (2d) 177, 346 P. (2d) 999 (1959)

(Decided by the Supreme Court of Washington)

[This was an action by a school district to review a prior dependency order with the view in end of requiring the parents of a minor child to comply with the compulsory-attendance law. This law required all children between the ages of six and sixteen to be in attendance at either a public or private school. When the Wolds —parents of the child in question—withdrew her from public school and did not enroll her in a private school, a petition was filed in juvenile court to have her adjudged a delinquent, because of her violation of the law. The parents' defense was that the child was being taught by her mother at home. As a further defense, they stated "that they were members of the Seventh Elect Church In Spiritual Israel; that eating meat, fish or fowl, listening to music, and dancing were forbidden by the tenets of their church, and that, to be present where meat, fish or fowl was served or music played violated their religious belief." On August 8, 1955, the juvenile court declared that the child was a delinquent child but permitted her to remain in the custody of her parents conditioned on their providing a method of educating her in conformity with state law. The Wolds disregarded the decision of the court and, on May 13, 1957, the district again petitioned the juvenile court for a review of its dependency order of August 8, 1955. The court found that the facts which caused the court to render the existing order still existed. It also found that the mother's teaching methods had improved and, since the child was receiving an education comparable to that provided by the public schools, she was attending the equivalent of a private school as contemplated by the law. Following the entry of judgment, the district was granted a review by the Supreme Court. Here, the court reversed the decision of the lower court. It held that, because the mother did not hold a teaching certificate, the education given the child was not of a type approved by statute. In arriving at its decision it also ruled that the parents were not exempt from the application of the compulsory-attendance law "because school attendance is repugnant to their religion."]

OTT, Judge.

. . . .

The juvenile court's decision is inconsistent with State v. Counort, 1912, 69 Wash. 361, 124 P. 910, 41 L.R.A., N.S., 95 (to which decision we adhere), wherein this court held that a father teaching his children at home was doing so in violation of the compulsory school attendance law. In the cited case, this court said [69 Wash. at page 363, 124 P. at page 911]:

". . . We do not think that the giving of instruction by a parent to a child, conceding the competency of the parent to fully instruct the child in all that is taught in the public schools, is within the meaning of the law 'to attend a private school.' Such a requirement means more than home instruction. It means the same character of school as the public school, a regular, organized and existing institution, making a business of instructing children of school age in the required studies and for the full time required by the laws of this state. . . ."

. . . .

Although the trial court found that there are no legislative standards governing private schools in this state, such a conclusion is not supported by law. A school is an institution consisting of a teacher and pupils, irrespective of age, gathered together for instruction in any branch of learning. . . . The three essential elements of a school are (1) the teacher, (2) the pupil or pupils, and (3) the place or institution. If the alleged school has no teacher, then it does not qualify as a school. There is one standard which the legislature made applicable to all schools, both public and private, and that standard is that the teacher must be qualified to teach and hold a teaching certificate. . . .

. . . .

The Wolds had the place and the pupil, but not a teacher qualified to teach in the state of Washington. Their alleged private school did not legally qualify as such.

. . . .

In the instant case, the Wolds' alleged private school did not have a qualified teacher. The Wolds did not report that their daughter was attending a private school, nor did they attempt in any manner to qualify their alleged school as a private school with the person whose duty it was to exercise his discretion in granting the waiver to students of public school attendance.

We find no merit in the contention of the Wolds that they are excused from the penalties of the compulsory school attendance law because school attendance is repugnant to their religion. . . .

Although the freedom to believe remains absolute, religious beliefs, whatever they may be, are not a legal justification for violation of positive law. . . .

Guides for Class Discussion

1. Compare this case with *Commonwealth* v. *Renfrew, infra.*
2. How do you think the court would have held if the mother had held an appropriate teaching certificate granted by the state? Would it have overruled the case it cited—*State* v. *Counort?*

5. *"As a rule, parents [charged with violating a compulsory-attendance law] will not be permitted to set up the defense that the law is in violation of their religious principles" (p. 3).*

COMMONWEALTH V. RENFREW,
332 Mass. 492, 126 N. E. (2d) 109 (1955)
(Decided by the Supreme Judicial Court of Massachusetts, Suffolk)

[When parents allegedly failed to send their child to a public or private school or have him instructed in an approved manner, as required by statute, charges were brought against them. The lower court entered a judgment of conviction. Defendants excepted and the higher court overruled the exceptions. One ground on which defendants attempted to defend their actions was that, because they were Buddhists, such practices as Bible reading violated their religious convictions.]

RONAN, Justice.

. . . .

None of the various other enumerated admitted facts constituted any defence to these complaints. Home education of their child by the defendants without the prior approval of the superintendent or the committee did not show a compliance with the statute and bar the prosecution of the complaints. . . . *The right to religious freedom is not absolute.* [Emphasis supplied.] For instance, the refusal of the one in control of a minor of school age to have him vaccinated or to procure a physician's certificate that he is an unfit subject for vaccination on account of the defendant's religious belief, thus preventing the child from attending school, is no defence to a violation of the compulsory school attendance law. . . . The defendants and their child were Buddhists. . . . Another grievance of the defendants is that some things that he was taught were causing conflict with the principles of Buddhism although they conceded that these principles were in no way in conflict with the law. There is no specification whatever as to what were "some of the things" just mentioned. They may well have been the secular subjects ordinarily taught in the public schools. The defendants state that their child has been taught the Twenty-Third Psalm and the Lord's Prayer. The mere reading of the Bible and the recital of the Lord's Prayer in the public schools do not justify the failure of the defendants to have him attend school. For more than a century our statute has provided that a portion of the Bible shall be read daily in the public schools without written note or comment and that no pupil shall be required to take any personal part in the reading if his parent or guardian informs the teacher in writing that he has conscientious scruples against the pupil participating in such reading. . . . The purpose and validity of such a statute were explained and upheld, as was a regulation of a school committee that the schools should be opened each morning with a reading from the Bible and the offering of prayer, in Spiller v. Inhabitants of Woburn, 12 Allen 127. We think the case cited is in accord with the weight of authority. We cite a few of the decisions.

In view of what has been said there is no need to discuss the other exceptions including those taken to the denial of the motion for a new trial.

Exceptions overruled.

Guides for Class Discussion

1. Compare this case with *State* v. *Superior Court, supra;* and *Schempp* v. *Board of Education, infra.*
2. Do you think the defendant might have won his case if he had relied on the First Amendment to the Constitution of the United States which guarantees religious liberty?

3. Likewise, do you think reliance on the Fourteenth Amendment which forbids the state from enacting any law that abridges the privileges of citizens, would have been to his benefit?

6. ". . . *courts agree that the domicile of the child [for school purposes] is the domicile of the parents . . . [and, in general] it is sufficient if . . . [the child] is actually residing in the district for some other reason than to take advantage of its educational opportunities*" (p. 3).

Lewis v. Holden,
118 Vt. 59, 99 A. (2d) 758 (1953)
(Decided by the Supreme Court of Vermont)

[This action was brought to review a decision of the commissioner of education determining the residence, for school-attendance purposes, of petitioner's nephew. The boy, 16 years of age, went to reside with his uncle in Northfield, Vermont, in June, 1952. He was entered in the high school there, but the defendant school board and superintendent notified plaintiff that, because he did not have legal control over the boy, the town of Northfield would not be responsible for his tuition. Thereupon, the father of the boy signed a written instrument relinquishing all control over him and vesting the boy's care, custody, and control in the hands of the uncle. The agreement was not acceptable to the board, and petitioner then requested, as he was entitled to do by statute, the commissioner of education to rule on the residence of the boy. The commissioner ruled that his residence was that of his father in Montpelier, and this action was brought. The court upheld the decision of the commissioner.]

CLEARY, Justice.

. . . .

The second issue is whether the agreement of the father placed the legal control of the minor in the petitioner. . . . However this is decided ie petitioner contends that a third issue is the proper interpretation of iis statute and says the history of the statute should be considered. Previous to 1927 the statute read: "the residence of a pupil is where ie person having control of him resides." The Legislature of 1927 mended it by adding the word "legal" before the word "control" to ead as it does now. Acts of 1927 No. 30. The petitioner offers no explanation of the amendment except to suggest that the addition of the ord very well may have been made by a draftsman through inadvertence. But we cannot assume that it was placed in the act inadvisedly nd without legislative intent that it should be given meaning and force i the application of the law. . . .

. . . .

"Legal" may mean "lawful" . . . ; it means "done according to law" . . . Black also defines "legal" as "conforming to law; required or permitted by law; good and effectual in law." . . . We think the plain meaning of the word as used in the statute in question here is lawful ontrol, that is control according to law. . . .

Using that definition the petitioner did not have such control that his residence was the residence of the minor for school purposes. He was either parent, foster parent nor guardian, and the minor was not pprenticed to him.

The petitioner devotes considerable space to the argument that the written instrument in question is valid and says the test to be applied s whether the agreement is favorable or unfavorable to the interests f the infant. . . .

The petitioner contends that whether a person has "legal control" of child, for school purposes and within the meaning of V.S. 47, § 4308 hould depend upon two things: first, that the change in residence by he minor be permanent and not for educational purposes only, and second, that after the change in residence the child be under the complete care, control and custody of the person with whom the minor has aken up residence. The Legislature in the statute has prescribed otherwise; not that legal control shall depend on the residence of the minor but that the residence of the minor for school purposes shall depend in the residence of the person having legal control of the pupil.

The petitioner admits that one is entitled to no consideration where child has been placed in some other town merely for the purpose of attending school in such town. The effect is the same where the change of legal control was made merely for that purpose. The instrument of transfer was not made until after the superintendent of schools had notified the petitioner that the Town of Northfield would not be responsible for the minor's tuition because the petitioner did not have legal control of the minor. The petitioner does not question that the decision of the school board in the first instance was proper or that the legal control of the minor at that time was in his parent. Petitioner's counsel admitted in oral argument that the so-called "Indenture" was made to meet the refusal of the school board to allow the minor to attend school

tuition free. Under such circumstances it was not binding upon the de
fendants in determining the residence of the minor for school purpose
. . . It was void as being against public policy because it was injuriou
to the interests of the public and contravened an established intere:
of society. . . .

Guides for Class Discussion

1. If education is a state function, how can this decision b
   defended?
2. If it had been shown that the boy had gone to live with th
   uncle for some reason other than that of attending school i
   Northfield, how do you think the court would have ruled?
3. Is this decision equitable? Give reasons.

7. *"The fact that a parent owns property and pays taxes in*
district in which he does not reside does not entitle him to sen
his children to the schools of that district free of tuition" (p. 4:

LOGAN CITY SCHOOL DISTRICT v. KOWALLIS,
94 Utah 342, 77 P. (2d) 348 (1938)
(Decided by the Supreme Court of Utah)

[This was an action to enjoin certain children from attending
the public schools of the Logan, Utah, city school district, unti
tuition fees had been paid. The children, who came from tw
separate families, were nonresidents of the district. Their parent:
lived just outside the district and, in both cases, were businessmer
and substantial taxpayers within the City of Logan. Because o:
this fact the parents insisted the children should be permitted t
attend the schools of Logan. The lower court granted the injunctior
prayed for. The higher court affirmed the decision of the lowe:
court.]

LARSON, Justice.

. . . Karl A. Kowallis, defendant, operates a printery within Logar

City, spends most of his time there, and is a substantial taxpayer within the city. Defendant Noah A. Larsen conducts within Logan City a retail hardware establishment and is a heavy taxpayer. . . .

. . . .

The requirement that the schools must be open to all children of the state is a prohibition against any law or rule which would separate or divide the children of the state into classes or groups, and grant, allow, or provide one group or class educational privileges or advantages denied another. No child of school age, resident within the state, can be lawfully denied admission to the schools of the state because of race, color, location, religion, politics, or any other bar or barrier which may be set up which would deny to such child equality of educational opportunities or facilities with all other children of the state. This is a direction to the Legislature to provide a system of public schools to which all children of the state may be admitted. It is also a prohibition against the Legislature, or any other body, making any law or rule which would deny admission to, or exclude from, the public schools any child resident of the state, for any cause except the child's own conduct, behavior, or health. The schools are open to all children of the state when there are no restrictions on any child, children, or group of children which do not apply to all children in the state alike. The provision for being open does not apply to matters financial; it does not mean they must be free. It simply means that all children must have equal rights and opportunity to attend the grade or class of school for which such child is suited by previous training or development.

. . . .

Since each district is charged with the duty of providing adequate school facilities for the children resident in the district, in order that such children may not be deprived of school privileges by overcrowding of rooms, or too large attendance for the book or laboratory facilities, or imposing too many students on a teacher for efficient work, the district must have the privilege of barring nonresident students whose home district provides for them proper educational advantages. . . .

. . . .

Appellants' contention that, although they reside outside the boundaries of the Logan City School District, they should for school purposes be considered as residents of the city, is likewise without merit.

Guides for Class Discussion

1. Compare this case with *State* v. *Jackson, supra.*
2. In this case the district of residence had adequate schools. Do you think the court would have held as it did if the schools had not been adequate?

3. If the parents had paid no taxes whatsoever in the district of residence, as was possible, but paid all of their taxes to the city school district, do you think the decision would have been equitable?

8. ". . . *statutes [that provide that children may attend school in districts in which they are nonresidents have generally] been held [to] . . . violate the principle of uniformity of taxation, unless they provide that the home district of the pupil shall pay a proportionate share of the cost of school maintenance in the district to which the pupil is transferred*" (p. 4).

High-School District v. Lancaster County,
60 Neb. 147, 82 N.W. 380 (1900)
(Decided by the Supreme Court of Nebraska)

[This action involved the constitutionality of a law that provided for the free attendance at public high schools of nonresident pupils. It also provided that an arbitrary sum be paid out of the general fund of the county as compensation to the district for the cost of tuition of such pupils. When a high school district filed a claim against the county for the tuition for nonresident pupils enrolled in its high school, and the county refused to pay, this action was brought. The defendant demurred on the ground the law was unconstitutional, and its action was sustained. Plaintiff then appealed and the higher court upheld the decision of the lower court.]

Norval, C. J.

. . . .

Before entering at large upon the discussion of the questions presented by the record, we would say that it does not appear to the court that the constitutional objections urged against this act are in any wise mitigated by the provision in section 3 thereof which grants to the school district, as compensation for the tuition of such nonresident pupils, the fixed and arbitrary sum therein named. Such sum may fall below, or exceed, the cost of such tuition, and is therefore not a factor tending to mitigate or off-set any objections that are raised in the case. So far as it affects the question, the act may have as well provided that such tuition might be without cost to a taxpayer resident outside such school districts. An act providing that non-resident pupils should be taught free of cost to taxpayers outside the limits of the district would, in our opinion, violate section 4 of article 9 of the constitution, for it would, in effect, release from their proportionate share of the taxes necessary to pay the cost of tuition of such non-resident pupils all portions of the county lying outside the limits of such high school district, and would be taxing one portion of a county for the benefit of another portion. . . .

. . . It will be observed that section 1 of the constitution, quoted, prescribes among other things, substantially, that the legislature shall provide such revenue as may be needful, by levying a tax by valuation, so that every person and corporation shall pay a tax in proportion to the value of his, her or its property and franchises, etc. Section 6 provides, substantially, that, for all corporate purposes, except certain ones therein enumerated, all municipal corporations may be invested with authority to assess and collect taxes, but such taxes shall be uniform in respect to persons and property within the jurisdiction of the body imposing the same; and section 4 prohibits the legislature from releasing or discharging any county, city, township, town or district whatever, or the inhabitants thereof, or any corporation, or the property therein, from their or its proportionate share of the taxes to be levied for state purposes, or due any municipal corporation, and from commuting any such taxes, in any form whatever. . . .

. . . .

We quite agree with counsel for plaintiff that, under this act, the county is the proper unit of taxation; but we have already shown that, in event the cost of tuition should exceed or fall below the amount provided by section 3 of the act to be raised by taxing the property of the whole county, it would indirectly violate the rule of uniformity prescribed in section 6 of the article of the constitution named. It would also violate section 4 of said article, as an advantage would accrue to the taxpayers resident in the one or the other of the two portions of the county affected thereby, and it would clearly be a commutation of the taxes to be paid by the taxpayers resident in the one or the other of the two localities. . . . It would seem clear and convincing that the act violates the provisions of the constitution cited, in the respects named, and that legislation of the character of the act in question cannot be upheld by the court.

Guides for Class Discussion

1. Would the court have held as it did if the law had provided that the county pay the actual cost of tuition rather than a fixed, arbitrary sum?

2. Compare this case with *Lewis* v. *Holden, supra.*
3. How can this decision be defended in light of the fact that the legislature has plenary control over education?

9. *"Pupils living in territory under the exclusive jurisdiction of the United States government are not entitled to attend the schools of the community free of tuition"* (p. 4).

Schwartz v. O'Hara Township School District,
375 Pa. 440, 100 A. (2d) 621 (1953)
(Decided by the Supreme Court of Pennsylvania)

[This was an action in mandamus to require a school district and its officers to furnish free educational facilities to children who resided within the district on the grounds of a Veterans Administration hospital. The district refused to admit the children in question to its schools, or to pay their tuition to the schools of another district, on the ground that the exclusive jurisdiction of the land on which they resided had been vested in the United States government. The lower court ruled against the plaintiffs, and the higher court upheld the judgment of the lower court.]

Jones, Justice.

.   .   .   .

The appellant's further contention is that the children here under consideration are residents of the O'Hara Township School District within the meaning of the Pennsylvania Public School Code of 1949, Act of March 10th, P.L. 30, 24 P.S. § 1-101 et seq., and are, therefore, entitled to attend the Township's schools free of charge. In support of this contention the appellant cites Sec. 1301 of the Pennsylvania School Code, 24 P.S. § 13-1301, which declares that "Every child, being a resident of any school district, . . . may attend the public schools in his district, . . ." and Sec. 1302 which provides that "A child shall be considered a resident of the school district in which his parents or the guardian of his person resides." But, neither the parents nor the guardians of these children reside in O'Hara Township. To be a resident of a particular political subdivision of a State a person must reside on land over which the State has jurisdiction. It has long been held that persons living on Federal reservations are not residents of the States wherein such reservations are situated. In the present instance, the Federal Government has exclusive jurisdiction of the area of O'Hara Township on which the Veterans Administration Hospital is located. . . . Nor is such jurisdiction impaired in the slightest degree by reason of the minor reservation in the act of cession of concurrent State jurisdiction merely for service of process. In Fort Leavenworth Railroad Co. v. Lowe, supra, the Supreme Court said, 114 U. S. at pages 532-533, 5 S.Ct. at page 999, "When the title is acquired by purchase by consent of the legislatures of the states, the federal jurisdiction is exclusive of all state authority. This follows from the declaration of the constitution that congress shall have 'like authority' over such places as it has over the district which is the seat of government; that is, the power of 'exclusive legislation in all cases whatsoever.' Broader or clearer language could not be used to exclude all other authority than that of congress; and that no other authority can be exercised over them has been the uniform opinion of federal and state tribunals, and of the attorney general."

Guides for Class Discussion

1. How do you think the court would have ruled if the federal government had not had exclusive jurisdiction over the territory involved?

2. What recourse do children such as those involved in this case have when denied educational opportunities in local schools?

3. Is this decision in the interest of free and universal education? Give reasons.

10. *"The Supreme Court of the United States has ruled that to deny a pupil the right to attend the public school of his choice because of race or color violates the equal-protection-of-the-law clause of the Fourteenth Amendment"* (p. 4).

BROWN V. BOARD OF EDUCATION OF TOPEKA,
347 U. S. 483 (1954)
(Decided by the Supreme Court of the United States)

[The Fourteenth Amendment of the federal constitution, which provides that "no state shall . . . deny to any person within its jurisdiction the equal protection of the laws," constitutes a type of limitation on the authority of the states. In interpreting this section, it has been held that a state may not enact and enforce rules or laws that discriminate against one class of citizens. The best known case in which this amendment has been interpreted or applied is *Brown* v. *Board of Education*, in which the United States Supreme Court ruled that states could not enact laws having the effect of segregating races in public schools.]

MR. CHIEF JUSTICE WARREN delivered the opinion of the Court.

. . . .

Today, education is perhaps the most important function of state and local governments. Compulsory school attendance laws and the great expenditures for education both demonstrate our recognition of the importance of education to our democratic society. It is required in the performance of our most basic public responsibilities, even service in the armed forces. It is the very foundation of good citizenship. Today it is a principal instrument in awakening the child to cultural values, in preparing him for later professional training, and in helping him to adjust normally to his environment. In these days, it is doubtful that any child may reasonably be expected to succeed in life if he is denied the opportunity of an education. Such an opportunity, where the state has undertaken to provide it, is a right which must be made available to all on equal terms.

We come then to the question presented: Does segregation of children in public schools solely on the basis of race, even though the physical facilities and other "tangible" factors may be equal, deprive the children of the minority group of equal educational opportunities? We believe that it does.

In *Sweatt* v. *Painter, supra,* in finding that a segregated law school for Negroes could not provide them equal educational opportunities, this Court relied in large part on "those qualities which are incapable

of objective measurement but which make for greatness in a law school."
In *McLaurin* v. *Oklahoma State Regents*, [339 U. S. 637], *supra*, the
Court, in requiring that a Negro admitted to a white graduate school
be treated like all other students, again resorted to intangible considerations: ". . . his ability to study, to engage in discussions and ex-
change views with other students, and, in general, to learn his profession." Such considerations apply with added force to children in grade
and high schools. To separate them from others of similar age and
qualifications solely because of their race generates a feeling of in-
feriority as to their status in the community that may affect their hearts
and minds in a way unlikely ever to be undone. . . .

We conclude that in the field of public education the doctrine of
"separate but equal" has no place. Separate educational facilities are
inherently unequal. Therefore, we hold that the plaintiffs and others
similarly situated for whom the actions have been brought are, by
reason of the segregation complained of, deprived of the equal protection of the laws guaranteed by the Fourteenth Amendment. This
disposition makes unnecessary any discussion whether such segregation
also violates the Due Process Clause of the Fourteenth Amendment.

Guides for Class Discussion

1. What was meant by the "separate but equal" doctrine?
2. It has been stated that this case has the result of defining
   "equality" in terms of "identity." What is meant by this?
3. What applications does the case have to the problem of race
   relations?
4. What line of reasoning did the court follow?
5. What limitation does this case place upon the authority of the
   state with respect to education?

11. "*. . . lower federal courts have held that the Supreme Court decisions do not require integration but merely forbid the use of governmental force to enforce segregation. . . . What . . . [they] do require is that all pupils, regardless of race or color, have free access, if they so desire it, to the schools maintained by state authority*" (p. 4).

PETTIT v. BOARD OF EDUCATION OF HARFORD COUNTY,
184 F. Supp. 452 (1960)
(Decided by the United States District Court, D. Maryland)

[This was a school segregation case questioning the legality of the desegregation plan of the school board of Harford County, Maryland. It was brought to require the board to admit a Negro child to a grade other than the one to which he was admitted. In ruling in his favor, the court commented on the meaning of the *Brown* cases, which declared segregation of children by race and color unconstitutional.]

THOMSEN, Chief Judge.

. . . .

. . . The experience in Maryland, including Baltimore City, shows that different individuals, both Negro and white, desire different educational experiences. Some Negro parents have sent their children to predominantly white schools; a majority have sent their children to schools which are entirely or predominantly colored. Many white parents have enrolled their children in schools where a few or many Negroes have enrolled, although they could have sent them elsewhere. The evidence in this case shows that there are at least two white children in the Lemmel Junior High School in Baltimore, where all the other pupils are colored. The ratios vary from county to county, as would be expected in a state so diverse as Maryland. The people of Maryland believe in such freedom of choice. It has produced constantly increasing desegregation of both public and private facilities. . . .

In School Board of City of Charlottesville, Va. v. Allen, supra, the Fourth Circuit quoted with approval the apt language of Judge Bryan in one of the cases then under consideration: "It must be remembered that the decisions of the Supreme Court of the United States in Brown v. Board of Education, 1954 and 1955, 347 U. S. 483 (74 S. Ct. 686, 98 L. Ed. 873) and 349 U. S. 294 (75 S. Ct. 753, 99 L. Ed. 1083) do not compel the mixing of the different races in the public schools. No general reshuffling of the pupils in any school system has been commanded. The order of the Court is simply that no child shall be denied admission to a school on the basis of race or color. Indeed, just so a child is not through any form of compulsion or pressure required to stay in a certain school, or denied transfer to another school, because of his race or color, the school heads may allow the pupil, whether white or Negro, to go to the same school as he would have attended in the absence of the ruling of the Supreme Court. Consequently, compliance with that ruling may well not necessitate such extensive changes in the school system as some anticipate." 240 F. 2d at page 62.

Guides for Class Discussion

1. If the Supreme Court, in the *Brown* cases, did not require integration, what was its significance?
2. Compare this case with *Brown* v. *Board of Education, supra.*

12. *"The federal courts have also ruled that the transition from a discriminatory school system to a nondiscriminatory system need not necessarily be abrupt . . . but it must be made 'with all deliberate speed'"* (pp. 4-5).

AARON v. TUCKER,
186 F. Supp. 913 (1960)
(Decided by the United States District Court, E.D. Arkansas, W.D.)

[In this case the actions of the Little Rock, Arkansas, school board in making pupil assignments under a previously court-approved plan for integrating schools was questioned. The court held that the individual rights of certain pupils in question were not violated by the board's actions in denying them applications for reassignment.]

JOHN E. MILLER, District Judge, sitting by assignment.

. . . .

The law requires and the plan provides for a transition from a constitutionally discriminatory school system to a constitutionally nondiscriminatory school system. While this transition is in progress, we can not lose sight of the realities and practicalities of the situation. We are dealing with children and their education, and the courts must consider the constitutional rights of the child along with the requirements of the school systems, and whether such requirements correspond with or conflict with the wishes of some of the students and their parents. It is understandable that certain students, as well as their parents, may entertain an abstract view of their rights or welfare that is not shared by the local school officials, who must constantly, in the solution of the varied problems and during the transition period, keep before them the broader prospective of the rights of students and the requirements of the school system. This broader prospective, implemented in good faith, may well necessitate during the transition period a denial of the wishes of a particular child or his parents. In relation to the problem of general achievement the court is entitled to require that the enjoyment of the right to desegregation "be geared to a reasonable, definitive, transitional program of 'all deliberate speed.'"

Under the facts in the instant case, the defendants have made every attempt and, in fact, are following a transitional program with "all deliberate speed." The law does not require that the door be open for admission on a "first come, first served" basis. If it were otherwise, we would soon have no order and no school system.

The courts have often recognized that many individual liberties guaranteed by the Constitution are not and cannot be unlimited. For example, there is no such thing as complete freedom of the press or speech, nor is there an unlimited or unrestrained freedom of students, white or colored, to select and "crash" their way into a particular school under the guise of choosing the direction in which their constitutional advantages lie.

Aside from the strictly constitutional or legal point of view, dedicated school officials must be and are concerned with transition in the sense of making the change in a manner to reach the desired end result without destroying children and the system in the process, and to arrive at a state of operation of a constitutional school system wherein all children can get at least as good an education, and preferably better, as was available to them in the former school system. The closer the goal is approached, the more successful is the transition. Realistically, every one knows that the principal obstacles to the achievement of the ultimate goal arises because school boards are dealing with children with different backgrounds, race, academic achievement, emotional stability, ability to adjust emotionally under new and trying circumstances, and other relevant factors, rather than physical plant, teacher load, transportation, etc.

Guides for Class Discussion

1. What line of reasoning motivated the court?

2. Are you in agreement with the principle of "all deliberate speed"? Give reasons.
3. What constitutes "all deliberate speed"?

3. *"It is a generally accepted principle of law . . . that where the atutes provide administrative remedies these must be exhausted efore the courts will assume jurisdiction"* (p. 5).

CARSON V. WARLICK,
238 F. (2d) 724 (1956)
(Decided by the United States Court of Appeals, Fourth Circuit)

[This was an action in mandamus wherein it was alleged that he board of education was practising racial discrimination because : refused to admit plaintiffs to schools maintained in the town of)ld Fort, North Carolina. In an earlier case, plaintiffs asked for n injunction to require their admission to the schools. The lower ourt ruled that a pupil-enrollment act provided certain administrative remedies which plaintiff had not taken advantage of and so tayed proceedings until such remedies had been exhausted. This ction was then brought to require the District Judge to vacate the order staying proceedings and to proceed with the cause as though : pupil-enrollment act had never been enacted. The court here upheld the action of the lower court.]

PARKER, Chief Judge.

. . . .

We think it clear that applicants are not entitled to the writ of mandamus which they ask, for the reason that it nowhere appears that they nave exhausted their administrative remedies under the North Carolina Pupil Enrollment Act, and are not entitled to the relief which they seek n the court below until these administrative remedies have been exhausted. . . . In the supplemental complaint which they proposed to file in the court below they did, indeed, allege that on August 24, 1955, they had presented their children at the Old Fort school for admission, that they were denied admission on the ground of race and that on

August 27 they and certain other Negroes had filed a joint petition wi
the school board asking that their children be admitted to the scho
This petition was denied by the Board in January 1956 and it was
appeal from this order of the Board to the Superior Court and then
to the Supreme Court of the State in which the decision of the Suprem
Court of May 23, 1956 was rendered. While the presentation of t
children at the Old Fort school appears to have been sufficient as t
first step in the administrative procedure provided by statute, the pros
cution of a joint or class proceeding before the school board was n
sufficient under the North Carolina statute as the Supreme Court
North Carolina pointed out in its opinion; and not until the administr
tive procedure before the board had been followed in accordance wi
the interpretation placed upon the statute by that court would appl
cants be in position to say that administrative remedies had been e
hausted.

It is argued that the Pupil Enrollment Act is unconstitutional; but w
cannot hold that that statute is unconstitutional upon its face and th
question as to whether it has been unconstitutionally applied is n
before us, as the administrative remedy which it provides has not bee
invoked. It is argued that it is unconstitutional on its face in that
vests discretion in an administrative body without prescribing adequat
standards for the exercise of the discretion. The standards are set fort
in the second section of that act . . . and require the enrollment to b
made "so as to provide for the orderly and efficient administration o
such public schools, the effective instruction of the pupils therein e
rolled, and the health, safety, and general welfare of such pupils'
Surely the standards thus prescribed are not on their face insufficient t
sustain the exercise of the administrative power conferred. . . .

Somebody must enroll the pupils in the schools. They cannot enro
themselves; and we can think of no one better qualified to undertake th
task than the officials of the schools and the school boards having th
schools in charge. It is to be presumed that these will obey the law
observe the standards prescribed by the legislature, and avoid the di
crimination on account of race which the Constitution forbids. Not unt
they have been applied to and have failed to give relief should th
courts be asked to interfere in school administration. . . .

Guides for Class Discussion

1. Compare this case with *Parham* v. *Dove, infra.*
2. What is the significance of the principle which this cas
   illustrates?
3. What line of reasoning did the court follow in arriving at it
   decision?

4. "Where [pupil-assignment statutes are based on] . . . *criteria
[hat] are reasonable and not based on race or color, the courts
[h]ld the statutes constitutional on their face*" (p. 5).

PARHAM V. DOVE,
271 F. (2d) 132 (1959)
(Decided by the United States Court of Appeals, Eighth Circuit)

[This action was brought by Negro pupils to compel admission
[t]o white schools. The lower court entered judgment from which
[b]oth plaintiffs and defendants appealed. The court, here, declared
[th]at the Arkansas Pupil Placement Act of 1959 was not unconsti-
[t]utional on its face and could not be so applied as to continue or
[p]romote segregation.]

JOHNSEN, Chief Judge.

.   .   .   .

. . . so far as the face of the statute is concerned, there is no basis to
[s]ay, in legal construction, that the Act is designed, or that it can only
[o]perate, to maintain segregation and to prevent integration in a school
[s]ystem. On the other hand, as emphasized in the Shuttlesworth case,
[1]62 F. Supp. at page 384, the statute cannot, because of its facial con-
[s]titutionality, be made to serve through artificial application, as an in-
[s]trument for maintaining or effecting a system of racial segregation. It
[c]annot be given an application designed to escape or by-pass the Brown
[c]ases. Recognition of and obedience to the holdings of the Brown cases
[m]ust implicitly exist in its operation and application.

Accordingly, any scrutiny which the federal courts may be called
[u]pon to make of what has been done under such a statute, where a
[c]harge of racial discrimination is involved, must necessarily be within
[t]he focus and tests of its lack of disharmony with the objective, the
[o]bligation and the responsibility dictated by the Brown cases. Insofar
[a]s the question of desegregation is concerned, a placement or assign-
[m]ent statute, such as the Arkansas Act, is entitled to have play, on the
[b]asis of state sovereignty, as a means or an aid for effecting a sound and
[o]rderly distribution of pupils, in relation to all the problems of a public
[s]chool system, except those of purely racial consideration. . . .

In this field of constitutional paramountcy, a placement or assign-
[m]ent statute is entitled to be accorded recognition only as an implement
[o]r adjunctive element on the part of a state for effecting an orderly
[s]olution to its desegregation difficulties, in proper relationship to its
[o]ther school-system problems, but with a subservience to the supreme-
[l]aw declaration of the Brown cases as to all imposed segregation and

the obligation owed to get rid thereof within the tolerance entitled
be allowed play under these decisions for accomplishing that result.

But there is no need here to extend further these generalized observ
tions. Reverting to the facial constitutionality of the Placement Act,
follows that the plaintiffs are without any general public-school rig
under Arkansas law to seek admission to a particular school, except
the basis of and in accordance with the provisions of that Act. Wh
their federal constitutional rights have been previously violated in th
they have been required to attend a school segregated under admini
trative authority, the Placement Act provides a means for them no
to seek admission to the school which they think they are otherwi
entitled to attend and, insofar as the provisions of the Act are co
cerned, have their right to do so determined without regard to the
race or color.

Guides for Class Discussion

1. Does this decision mean that federal courts will have no con
   cern with the consitutionality of pupil-assignment laws?
2. Does this decision authorize the states to enact pupil-assign
   ment laws that operate on the basis of race and color?
3. Compare this case with *Carson* v. *Warlick, supra.*

15. *"School attendance is a privilege extended by the state an
not an absolute right . . ." (p. 5).*

BISSELL v. DAVISON,
65 Conn. 183, 32 A. 348 (1894)
(Decided by the Supreme Court of Errors of Connecticut)

[This was an action for a writ of mandamus brought by the
parent of a child against the school committee of the town of New
Britain to require it to admit his minor son as a pupil in the high
school. The school committee had enacted a rule requiring vaccination as a prerequisite to admission to school. Under this rule
the plantiff's son was excluded from school solely because of his
refusal to be vaccinated, whereupon this action was brought. Plain-

ff based his action mainly on the contention that the board rule
'as unconstitutional under the Fourteenth Amendment to the
ational constitution, as well as under the constitution of the state.
'he lower court ruled in favor of the board, and the higher court
pheld the decision of the lower court. In arriving at its decision,
ie higher court noted that a child has no right to attend school, but
stead, attendance is a privilege.]

TORRANCE, J. . . .

.   .   .   .

The plaintiff contends that the statute conferring the power to re-
uire vaccination as a condition of admittance to or attendance at the
ublic schools violates certain provisions of the constitution of this
tate, and of the fourteenth amendment to the national constitution. He
ays, in effect, that it allows the privileges of the common schools to
hose who believe in vaccination, and denies it to those who do not;
hat it deprives him of his rights, without due course or process of law,
nd denies to him the equal protection of the laws. These objections
o the validity of the statute, and the reasons and arguments urged in
upport of them, seem to proceed upon a misconception or misapprehen-
ion of the real nature and object of the statute. The statute in ques-
ion forms a part of the laws relating to our common-school system, and
nust be read as a part of those laws. The duty of providing for the
education of the children within its limits, through the support and
maintenance of public schools, has always been regarded in this state
n the light of a governmental duty resting upon the sovereign state. It
s a duty not imposed by constitutional provision, but has always been
assumed by the state; not only because the education of youth is a
matter of great public utility, but also, and chiefly, because it is one of
great public necessity for the protection and welfare of the state itself.
In the performance of this duty, the state maintains and supports, at
great expense, and with an ever-watchful solicitude, public schools,
throughout its territory, and secures to its youth the privilege of attendance therein. This is a privilege or advantage, rather than a right,
in the strict technical sense of the term. This privilege is granted, and
is to be enjoyed, upon such terms and under such reasonable conditions and restrictions as the law-making power, within constitutional
limits, may see fit to impose; and, within those limits, the question what
terms, conditions, and restrictions will best subserve the end sought in
the establishment and maintenance of public schools is a question solely
for the legislature, and not for the courts. The statute in question
authorizes the committee to impose vaccination as one of those conditions. It does not authorize or compel compulsory vaccination. It
simply requires vaccination as one of the conditions of the privilege of attending the public school. Its object is to promote the usefulness and

efficiency of the schools by caring for the health of the scholars. . .
In the case at bar the required condition is made to operate impartial
upon all children alike. It affects all in the same way, and reasonab
provision is made for providing free vaccination where necessary. It
a reasonable exercise of the power to require vaccination, if such r
quirement ever can, in the nature of things, be a reasonable one. .
vaccination is a preventive of smallpox, as claimed by what appears t
be the great majority of the medical profession, the requirement wou.
seem to be a reasonable one. Public opinion, also, upon this question
as crystallized into law, seems to regard it as such a preventive. . .
The question before us is not whether the legislature ought to hav
passed such a law. It is simply whether it had the power to pass i
In no proper sense can this statute be said to contravene the provision
of section 1 of the first article of our state constitution, as claimed b
the plaintiff. It may operate to exclude his son from school, but, if s
it will be because of his failure to comply with what the legislatur
regards, wisely or unwisely, as a reasonable requirement, enacted i
good faith to promote the public welfare. Nor, in any proper sense
can the statute be said to deprive the plaintiff of any right without du
process of law, or to deny to him the equal protection of the law.

We think the demurrer was properly overruled. There is no error
The other judges concurred.

Guides for Class Discussion

1. Compare this case with *Anderson* v. *State, infra.*
2. How would you distinguish between the terms "right" and
   "privilege"?
3. What is the real significance of this decision?

16. *"School boards have the authority to classify pupils on the
basis of scholarship"* (p.5).

BOARD OF EDUCATION V. STATE,
88 Ohio St. 133, 88 N.E. 412 (1909)
(Decided by the Supreme Court of Ohio)

[This was an action in mandamus against a board of education
to compel it to admit a certain boy into the seventh grade. The
preceding year the boy had passed his examinations in the fifth
grade and had been promoted into the sixth grade. The board had

very detailed rules for the administration of the school, including certain rules concerning the nature and time of examinations. When school opened in the fall of 1907 the boy, without the knowledge or consent of the board or superintendent, presented himself for enrollment in the seventh grade. There he remained for four days. When the superintendent found that he had enrolled in the seventh grade, he informed him that, because he had been promoted to the sixth grade, he would have to register there. The boy immediately left school and did not return. Shortly after, his father brought this action in the name of the state to compel the board to admit the boy to the seventh grade. He contended the boy had been tutored during the summer and had made such satisfactory progress that he was qualified to do the work of that grade. When the cause was tried in the lower court, the court had the boy examined by a superintendent of schools. The superintendent reported the boy was qualified to do seventh-grade work, and the lower court ordered the board to admit the pupil to that grade. The school board appealed. The higher court overruled the lower court.]

Spear, J. . . .

.   .   .   .

It is manifest from the whole record that the circuit court acted upon the belief that the question whether or no the pupil was fitted to enter the seventh grade, and should have been promoted from the fifth to the seventh, was rightfully to be determined by the court rather than by the school authorities. But is this the law? Section 4017, Rev. St. provides that the board shall have the management and control of all the public schools in the district. Section 3985 makes provision for the adoption of rules and regulations. . . . Following this authority, the board had made and promulgated rules and regulations as hereinbefore given. These rules seem to well cover the case in hand and to be appropriate to the objects intended. . . .

The complaint in the present case is that the application of some of these rules to this pupil worked an injustice, in that it denied him the right secured by section 4013, Rev. St., to freely enter the school of the district, and thereby deprived him of a right of promotion which because of his advanced proficiency he was entitled to enjoy, viz., to be promoted from the fifth to the seventh grade on the ground of merit. But who is empowered to judge of the merit and the proficiency? Is it the father of the child or the school authorities? The trial court seems to have assumed that in the first instance it is the father, and finally the court. . . . It is insisted in argument with great force and eloquence that the evidence conclusively shows that the boy was abundantly qualified to enter the seventh grade. The court, giving effect to all the evidence presented, so found, and we are not inclined to question that finding except to say that it was irrelevant to the real issue in the case. But the question is not what in fact were the qualifications of the boy, but what was the duty of the board on that Thursday evening when the situation as to the three pupils was called to its attention. The boy may have been qualified. Indeed, it appears from the whole case that the pupil was mentally a precocious boy. Whether it was best for the boy that he be thus crowded we need not inquire, though that consideration is sought to be impressed upon us pro and con. . . .

. . . By the testimony of the relator and his son it was made clear that the pupil was sent to the room of the seventh grade by his father and without permission of the school authorities. In other words, it was shown that he was an intruder. The willingness, if it existed at any time, of the superintendent that the boy should go to that room, could not avail, as the rule respecting promotions provided that they are to be made only, as conditions precedent, on the approval of the board based upon the recommendation of the teacher and superintendent. The testimony showed that neither condition obtained. . . .

It is insisted by relator's counsel that the board of education was composed of uneducated men, and hence was not qualified to judge of the merits of the pupil for promotion. We cannot know about that. It is enough to know that the statutes impose the duty on such boards, they having the aid afforded by the teachers and superintendent, and, if in any instance they are not qualified for the performance of such duty, it would become the voters of the district to elect men who would be qualified.

These conclusions require the reversal of the judgment of the circuit court and the dismissal of the petition at the costs of the relator, which judgment will be accordingly entered.

Reversed.

Guides for Class Discussion

1. How do you think the court would have held if it had been contended and proven that the board acted in an arbitrary manner?
2. What recourse would the parent have in a case of this sort?
3. Do you think that, by virtue of this decision, too much power is vested in the board of education?

17. "It has been held that pupils who are physically or mentally defective to the point that their presence would be harmful to other pupils may be excluded from the public schools" (p. 5).

MARTIN V. CRAIG,
42 N.D. 213, 173 N.W. 787 (1919)
(Decided by the Supreme Court of North Dakota)

[Plaintiff brought this case against the school district to compel the district to admit his children. The defendant district had barred them from admission on the ground that one of the children had been found "by a reputable physician and by a qualified representative of the federal health service" to be afflicted with trachoma, and that the other child was suspected of having it. During the preceding few years it appears that the disease had been prevalent in the county. The lower court refused the writ of mandamus, and the higher court affirmed the order of the lower court.]

BIRDZELL, J. . . .

The disease is communicable and of a very serious nature, frequently resulting in blindness and always in impairment of the normal functions of the tissues immediately affected. To prevent the spread of the disease and to secure proper treatment for those affected, the county board of health promulgated an order forbidding admission to school of children who, upon examination, were found to be or suspected of being afflicted, unless they were at the time under treatment for the disease.

In the instant case, the petitioner produced two doctors who presented what is generally considered to be first-class professional credentials qualifying them to give expert testimony. They had had ample opportunity to examine the patients and to diagnose the cases. In fact, the children had been patients of one of the doctors. These doctors testify that the children are not afflicted with trachoma but with folliculosis. One of them also testifies that it is injurious to the eye to treat it for trachoma when trachoma is not present, but a careful reading of his testimony discloses that the injury results from a species of treatment that is likely to be resorted to only when the disease is clearly present and when the necessity for radical treatment is indicated. . . .

The order of exclusion in the instant case cannot be said to be unreasonable. It only excludes those whose cases are positive and suspected, who are not at time under treatment. The seriousness of the disease and its communicable character afford ample foundation for such an order; and, even conceding that it may be doubted in the instant case whether the children in question are affected, the doubt is one that must be resolved in favor of the authorities charged with the serious responsibility of preventing the spread of the disease. This is a case where mandamus does not issue as a matter of right, but where it will only issue in the exercise of a judicial discretion, and this discretion should not be exercised in a way that might result in needlessly exposing healthful children to a disease as serious as trachoma. . . .

The order appealed from is affirmed.

Guides for Class Discussion

1. Compare this case with *Streich* v. *Board of Education, infra.*
2. In light of the fact that diagnoses here may have been questionable, do you agree with the court's reasoning? Give reasons.

18. *"Statutes authorizing local school boards to provide transportation of pupils to and from school have uniformly been held to be constitutional"* (p. 5).

Pasadena City High School District v. Upjohn,
206 Cal. 775, 276 P. 341 (1929)
(Decided by the Supreme Court of California)

[This was an action brought by a high school district to compel a county superintendent and auditor to approve and issue certain warrants ordered by the school district to pay for transportation services. The county superintendent and auditor refused to approve and allow certain of the warrants—that is, those covering items of expenditure for the transportation of pupils residing in the City of Sierra Madre which was a part of the plaintiff district. The question before the court was whether the board of education had the power to provide, at district expense, the transportation of these pupils. The board based its contention on the alleged unconstitutionality of an act which prohibited the board from transporting pupils living within the limits of any city. The defendants contended the act was constitutional. The lower court ruled in favor of the board, and the higher court affirmed its decision. It did so, not by declaring the act unconstitutional, but by interpreting it as applying only to pupils residing within a city in which was maintained a high school—*i.e.*, it held that because no high school was located in the City of Sierra Madre the board was not barred from transporting the pupils to high schools located within the City of Pasadena. In its decision the court found it necessary to comment on the authority of the legislature to enact laws providing for the transportation of pupils.]

SHENK, J. . . .

.   .   .   .

The contention of the respondents, that the furnishing of transportation as authorized by the statute is a gift of public money or thing of value in contravention of section 31 or article 4 of the Constitution, cannot be maintained. The state has a vital interest in the education of its youth. It furnishes free instruction, free text-books, and supplies, and builds and maintains buildings representing large investments. It recognizes the public duty to provide adequate and accessible school facilities not only for those who reside in populous centers, but also for those who reside in sparsely settled communities. The tendency to combine and enlarge high school districts in the interest of economy and proficiency is recognized. It seems reasonable to assume that training in our schools may best be accomplished by such centralization of educational facilities, and that greater economy may result by transporting the pupils residing in sparsely settled communities to a central high school than to expend large and perhaps unwarranted sums of money in constructing numerous high schools in such outlying sections. Our laws have provided for transportation to be given to school children for many years as a maintenance cost. . . . This has been done without question in the courts of this state on the ground that such provision is unconstitutional as a gift. In Veterans' Welfare Board v. Riley, 189 Cal. at page 161, 208 P. 679, 22 A. L. R. 1531, it was stated: "The plan of transporting school pupils to and from their homes, particularly in large union districts, is quite common in this state, and is expressly authorized by statute [citing the sections of the Political Code above noted]. . . . The validity of these sections of the code has not been questioned in the courts of this state."

.   .   .   .

The peremptory writ should therefore issue directing the respondents to approve and issue warrants for the payment of the claims presented by the petitioners covering the cost of transporting the high school pupils who reside in the city of Sierra Madre to and from said Pasadena city high school pursuant to the contract under which said transportation was furnished.

It is so ordered.

Guides for Class Discussion

1. Relate this case to the generally-accepted legal principle that, because education is a state function, the legislature has plenary control over it.

2. Under what conditions do you think defendants in this case might have prevailed in spite of the fact the act was constitutional?

19. *"Some courts have held that local school boards do not have the authority to spend public funds to provide transportation unless authorized to do so by statute . . ."* *(pp. 5-6).*

STATE EX REL. BEARD V. JACKSON,
168 Ind. 384, 81 N.E. 62 (1907)
(Decided by the Supreme Court of Indiana)

[This was an action in mandamus to compel a township trustee to furnish free transportation for certain pupils to and from a consolidated school in the township. It appears that a previous trustee had purchased suitable wagons for transporting pupils. The present trustee, however, refused to spend the funds to put these wagons into operation and to provide the transportation requested. There was no statute requiring that he provide transportation. The lower court refused to grant the writ of mandamus, and the higher court affirmed its decision.]

Montgomery, C. J. . . .

. . . .

. . . Our attention has not been directed to a statute specially enjoining the duty of providing free transportation for school children upon township trustees. . . . The official duties relevant to the question under consideration specified in the law are: "That the school trustees shall take charge of the educational affairs of their respective townships, towns and cities. They shall employ teachers, establish and locate conveniently a sufficient number of schools for the education of the children therein, and build or otherwise provide suitable houses, furniture, apparatus and other articles and educational appliances necessary for the thorough organization and efficient management of the schools." . . . No suggestion that free transportation of children be provided is here found; but on the contrary, it is commanded that a sufficient number of schoolhouses be provided and conveniently located for the education of the children. This statute also authorizes a township trustee to establish at least one separate graded high school in his township for advanced pupils, provided at least 25 common-school graduates of school age reside in the township. We are not required to consider either the wisdom or legality of the general consolidation of common schools shown by the complaint, but the inconvenience thus voluntarily occasioned can have little weight in construing general statutes prescribing the duties of school trustees of the state. The Constitution requires that provision be made by law "for a general and uniform system of common schools." Article 8, § 1, Const. Ind. If the duty to furnish free transportation to and from school is imposed upon appellee, a like obligation rests upon all other school trustees. The legal duty of appellee is not affected by the circumstance that his predecessor, with the concurrence of the advisory board, levied a tax to provide such transportation. . . .

. . . If the furnishing of such free transportation under the law be deemed expedient, the Legislature should enjoin the duty upon the appropriate officers, authorize the levy of adequate taxes to meet the expenses thereof, and prescribe the conditions and limitations under which the same is to be provided. . . . The requisite legislation cannot be supplied by the court, school officers, or local tribunals, but must emanate from the lawmaking body, and be general and uniform in its application.

Guides for Class Discussion

1. Compare this decision with *Foster* v. *Board of Education, infra.*
2. Can you reconcile the decision in the *Foster* case with the decision in this case?

3. How do you think the court would have held had there been
a statute permitting the township trustee to provide transportation?

20. *"[Some] . . . courts have held that school boards have the
implied authority to provide transportation"* (p. 6).

FOSTER v. BOARD OF EDUCATION,
131 Kan. 160, 289 P. 959 (1930)
(Decided by the Supreme Court of Kansas)

[This action was brought by a taxpayer for the purpose of obtaining an injunction against the defendant, Board of Education
of the City of Topeka, to prevent it from using tax funds to pay
for the transportation of certain pupils in the district. In the absence of statute permitting it to do so, the defendant entered into
a contract to furnish buses for the purpose of transporting pupils
from various parts of the city to certain specifically-mentioned
grade schools. One reason for so doing was to enroll Negro children,
regardless of where they lived, in Negro schools. In addition, the
district maintained a school for undernourished children, in which
were enrolled some forty children. These were also transported.
The lower court held in favor of the board, and the higher court
affirmed its decision.]

JOCHEMS, J.

. . . .

The appellant contends that the transportation of pupils is an extra-
ordinary function on the part of the school authorities not included
within the legitimate ends of education, and that a specific grant of
authority is a prerequisite to its exercise either in the case of common
school districts, community high schools, or boards of education in
cities of the first class. Appellant points out that country school districts and rural high school districts have been authorized by statute
to furnish transportation, but argues that the need for transportation

of pupils in country schools is much more pressing than in city school districts, and that, since the Legislature has seen fit to make an express grant of that power to country school districts, a similar express grant is necessary in order to authorize a board of education in a city of the first class to furnish transportation.

The appellee, on the other hand, relies on R. S. 72-1724, which reads: "The board of education shall have power to elect their own officers, make all necessary rules for the government of the schools of such city under its charge and control and of the board, subject to the provisions of this act and the laws of this state; to organize and maintain separate schools for the education of white and colored children, including the high schools in Kansas City, Kan.; no discrimination on account of color shall be made in high schools, except as provided herein; to exercise the sole control over the public schools and school property of such city."

Can it be said that the power to furnish transportation such as is being furnished by the board of education of the city of Topeka may be implied from the provisions of the foregoing statute? . . .

. . . .

As shown in the instant case, the city maintains nineteen schools for a total of 6,428 white children, or one school for an average of 338 pupils; it maintains four schools for 947 colored children, or one school for an average of 237 colored children. Having been granted specific power and authority by the statute to maintain separate schools, does it not necessarily follow that there must be an implication of authority to do all such acts as are reasonably necessary to enable the board of education to execute the power so expressly granted?

. . . .

This leaves the question of the authority to furnish transportation for the children who attend the school for the undernourished. The statute under consideration gives the board power to "make all necessary rules for the government of the schools of such city . . . and to exercise the sole control of the public schools and school property of such city."

. . . .

These children are undernourished and unable to mingle in the regular grade schools with those who are normal in every respect and to carry the work assigned to the physically normal children. In many instances if such a school is not maintained the child who is undernourished or physically weak could not attend school at all. We believe that, under the general powers granted to the board of education, it is necessarily implied that the board has power to provide means for the education of not only the children who are in all respects robust and physically sound, but also to provide facilities to those who are not so favored. The public welfare demands that the child who is not physically sound shall have an opportunity to gain a education the same as his more favored brother. We conclude there fore that the defendant board of education has the implied power an authority to furnish transportation both to the colored children and the undernourished children under the circumstances shown by th record in this case.

The injunction was properly denied, and the judgment is therefor affirmed.

Guides for Class Discussion

1. Compare this decision with *State ex rel. Beard* v. *Jackson supra.* Can they be reconciled?
2. Are you in agreement with the court's reasoning in this case Give reasons.

21. *"The courts will sustain the discretion of a school board in establishing and maintaining transportation routes and in determining what pupils will be transported, unless the board acts unreasonably and abuses its discretion"* (p. 6).

BOWEN V. MEYER,
255 S.W. (2d) 490 (Ky.) (1953)
(Decided by the Court of Appeals of Kentucky)

[This action was brought to require a board of education to provide transportation for elementary-school pupils who resided from one to two and one-quarter miles from school in certain suburban areas. The statute required boards of education to provide transportation for elementary school pupils "who do not reside within reasonable walking distance of the school provided for them." Here, the school building was located a little distance from the populated area. The board did not provide transportation, but pupils could ride public buses for a five to six and one-half cent fare. The lower court held that the board must provide ne transportation required, but the higher court reversed its ecision, holding that the board had not acted unreasonably or bused its discretion.]

CULLEN, Commissioner.

.   .   .   .

We think it is clear that the distance alone, which at the most is wo and one-quarter miles, is not unreasonable. . . .

In the case before us, the school is located on Westport Road, about 250 feet north of Hubbard Lane, which crosses Westport Road at ight angles. Massie Avenue lies some 1250 feet west of, and parallel vith, Westport Road, and Massie Avenue has its northern terminus at ts intersection with Hubbard Lane. Massie Avenue has a traffic count f one car every minute in the morning, and one car every two minutes n the afternoon. The traffic count on Westport Road is one car every 10 seconds in the morning, and one car every 20 seconds in the after- 100n. The morning traffic count on Hubbard Lane is one car every 15 seconds.

One group of school children would travel Massie Avenue on their vay to and from school. . . . It appears that . . . the only hazardous part of the route consists of that part of Massie Avenue running south from Hubbard Lane, a distance of 3250 feet. For some 2000 feet of this distance the pavement is from 11½ to 13 feet wide, with two or three-foot shoulders composed of gravel and tar with a somewhat uneven surface. For the remaining 1250 feet, the pavement is from 14 to 16 feet in width, with similar shoulders. On the part where the pavement is narrow, one car must pull off on the shoulder when meeting another car. There is no hazard other than the narrowness of the road.

The second group of children would travel Westport Road. At the southern end of the road they would be required to cross some rail- road tracks, on which two trains are scheduled in the morning, and two in the afternoon, at hours when the children might be passing. Westport Road has a pavement 22 feet in width, with three-foot shoulders covered with short grass and weeds. The distance the chil- dren would be required to walk along Westport Road is less than half a mile.

.   .   .   .

Another factor which we think may be given some consideration is the availability of common carrier bus transportation for the children, from their home neighborhoods to the intersection of Westport Road and Hubbard Lane, 1000 feet south of the school. The fare is five cents without transfer, and six and one-half cents with transfer. School safety patrol boys ride these buses to assist the younger children.

The board of education necessarily must be allowed some discretion in determining what is a reasonable walking distance in any particular

situation, and the courts should not interfere unless the board h
acted in an arbitrary and unreasonable manner in refusing to furni
transportation. . . .

We think the cricumstances here . . . and the hazards presented a
not of such magnitude as to make it mandatory upon the board
furnish transportation. Westport Road, itself, presents no unusu
dangers, and we do not consider the railroad tracks as being sufficien
alone, to require bus transportation to be supplied. Massie Avenue
narrow, it is true, but the traffic upon it is not heavy.

In a surburban area, such as this, children are exposed to the hazar
of traffic in any of their outdoor activities. They will be upon tl
streets in play, in visiting their friends, and in going to the store
They early in life must be trained to take care of themselves in traffi
Public bus transportation is a common convenience to them.

The situation of the surburban child is much different than that c
the country boy, who ordinarily is not upon the highways on foo
except in going to and from school; who is not conditioned to th
hazards of constant automobile traffic; and who has no means c
reaching school other than on foot or by school bus.

Guides for Class Discussion

1. Compare this case with *State* v. *Miller, infra.*
2. Do you agree with the court's consideration of traffic hazards
   as well as distance, in determining whether the board's policy
   was reasonable or not?
3. What assurance does a board have that the transportation
   policies it adopts are reasonable ones?

2. *"The courts will not require that conveyances be sent to the ome of each child or that transportation be provided for children ving in isolated or inaccessible places"* (p. 6).

STATE V. MILLER,
193 Ind. 492, 141 N.E. 60 (1923)
(Decided by the Supreme Court of Indiana)

[This was an action in mandamus brought by plaintiffs against a ownship trustee and the county superintendent of schools to re- uire them to have the school wagon driven to their homes to pick p school children. Plaintiffs lived in an abandoned school district, nd the trustee was transporting the children of school age to nother school in another district more than two miles away. The rustee had established a transportation route which required the hildren in question to walk approximately one-half to three- uarters of a mile to meet the school wagon. In making this trip, he children in question were required to cross a railroad, over vhich four regular passenger trains and six regular freight trains an daily. Plaintiffs alleged that on occasion the children had to wait rom five to twenty minutes for the school wagon and there was no helter for them at the intersection where they boarded it. The laintiffs had acquainted the trustee with the facts and requested im to change the route so that it would go past their homes, but e refused, and his refusal had been upheld by the county super- ntendent. The defendants demurred and the lower court upheld he demurrer. The higher court approved the action of the lower ourt.]

EWBANK, J. . . .

.   .   .   .

The . . . rule [that the law vests discretion in school officials] has been declared by the courts of other states in construing similar statutes. In a case in North Daktoa where the relator's sons, aged from 10 to 19 years, had been required to cross a small river that was frozen nearly all winter, and to walk a third of a mile to meet the school wagon, a judgment commanding that the wagon be driven some miles farther so as to pass the relator's door was reversed; the Supreme Court saying that although the duty of transporting the children was mandatory, a reasonable discretion was vested in the school board in determining how near to their homes the school wagon should be brought, and that the board had not abused its discretion in that instance. State ex rel. Mostad, 28 N. D. 244, 148 N. W. 831. And in a case in Ohio, where the father of a 13 year old girl petitioned for a writ commanding the township board of education to bring the school wagon to his door residence at a point where there was no shelter from cold and storm while waiting for it, the Supreme Court held that the acts complained of were within the discretion of the board as matters of administration and that its discretion could not be controlled by mandamus. State ex rel. v. Board of Education, 102 Ohio St. 446, 132 N. E. 16. And in Pennsylvania, where the relator and his children lived back on a private lane that connected with a crossroad one-half mile from an abandoned schoolhouse that stood beside the main road, and the officers of the school district required the children to walk down to the old schoolhouse and wait there for the wagon, a peremptory writ that had been awarded by the court of common pleas commanding the conveyance to be brought up to where relator's private lane entered the highway was set aside by the Supreme Court. Commonwealth ex rel v. Benton Twp., 277 Pa. 13, 120 Atl. 661. If there are any authorities holding the contrary, our attention has not been called to them.

The facts alleged in the complaint, together with any other pertinent facts, might properly be considered by the township trustee and the county superintendent in determining where the school wagon shall be driven. But so long as those officers are not shown to have abused the discretion vested in them by law, the courts cannot interefere to control their action. Whether it was better for four small children to cross the railroad twice each day on foot, or for a school wagon with children in it to be driven across four times each day, was a question for the officers to decide in laying out a route for the school wagon. No error was committed in sustaining a demurrer to the complaint.

The judgment is affirmed.

Guides for Class Discussion

1. Compare this decision with the one in *Bowen* v. *Meyer, supra.*
2. Compare this decision with the one in *Cross* v. *Fisher, infra.*
3. On what legal principle did the court base its decision?

. "In providing transportation for pupils, a board of education ust treat all who are in the same class or category alike" (p. 6).

CROSS v. FISHER,

132 Tenn. 31, 177 S.W. 43 (1915)

(Decided by the Supreme Court of Tennessee)

[This was an action by certain citizens, taxpayers, and patrons f a school district questioning the validity of an act permitting 1e consolidation of school districts under certain conditions and uthorizing the transportation of those who lived too far from 1e school to walk. Among other things, it was contended that 1e act was unconstitutional because, in providing for the transortation of certain pupils and not all, it conferred unequal priveges and benefits upon pupils. The lower court upheld the *egality of the act, and the higher court affirmed its decision.]

FANCHER, J. . . .

. . . .

But it is said that the act in question violates the Constitution because : only provides for the transportation of children who reside too far way from the school to attend without transportation, in case there is sufficient number of children so situated. This section of the act is as ollows:

"Be it further enacted, that whenever, by reason of such consolidaion, a sufficient number of children is situated too far away from such chools to attend without transportation, said boards of education are ereby . . . empowered to make provisions for the transportation of aid pupils that reside too far away from said school to attend without ransportation, and to pay for same out of the respective public school unds of the county in which such children reside."

The objection made to that part of this act which provides for ransportation of children is to the effect that, in the process of consoli-lation of schools, some of the children may live too far away to attend uch schools without transportation, and may be denied transportation because there is not a sufficient number in a given place or locality, and that this act on its face recognizes the right of a board to deny :ransportation to some.

It is further said that all people cannot live near schools nor trans-portation lines, and therefore it will not do to say that all citizens may or can bring themselves within a situation where they can enjoy the benefits of transportation under the act.

. . . .

The question then arises: Will this discrimination, or authority in th act to discriminate, subject this section of the act in question to th constitutional objections pointed out?

Section 12 of article 11 of the Constitution sets apart the intere on the common school fund to be used for the equal benefit of all th people of the state. But this does not mean that the schoolhouses sha be equally distant from every home, because that is impossible.

The inhibition against class legislation is clearly defined in sectio 8, art. 11, of the Constitution, and the provision in section 12 of sai article must be read in connection with the provisions of section 8.

The latter section provides that the Legislature shall have no powe to suspend any general law for the benefit of individuals inconsisten with the general laws of the land, nor to pass any law granting to an individual or individuals rights, privileges, immunities, or exemption other than such as may be by the same law extended to any membe of the community who may be able to bring himself within the pro visions of such law. So it is that, if any citizen may be able to brin himself within the provisions of a law, there is no discrimination withi the meaning of the Constitution.

Under section 2 of the said act there is no provision inconsistent wit this requirement of the Constitution, because any member of a com munity may be able to bring himself within the provision of the law.

Guides for Class Discussion

1. Compare the decision in this case with the one in *State v Miller, supra.*

2. What are the implications of this case for school administra tion today?

3. Are you in agreement with the court's thinking? Give reasons

4. *"School districts are not, as a rule, liable for injuries to pupils sustained while being transported to and from school, in the absence of a statute to the contrary"* (p. 6).

SCHORNACK V. SCHOOL DISTRICT,
64 S. D. 215, 266 N.W. 141 (1936)
(Decided by the Supreme Court of South Dakota)

[This was an action for damages for injuries received by a pupil as a result of the districts' alleged negligence in conducting the transportation program. The districts demurred, and the lower court sustained the demurrer. The higher court upheld the decision of the lower court.]

WARREN, Judge.

. . . .

Narrowed down to a specific statement of the law to be applied in this case in a decision upon the demurrer, it would seem that in doing the act complained of, the districts were either performing a governmental function, and it is the settled law that when school districts are performing governmental functions they cannot be held liable for negligence, or the act complained of exceeded the functions permitted to be exercised by school districts and the school officers were powerless by their conduct and acts to render the defendant districts liable for damages.

At the time of the alleged act of negligence, common school districts were vested with certain statutory power permitting them to transport pupils. . . . This court has held that independent school districts were also vested with such authority. . . . The complaint fails to sufficiently detail matters relative to and concerning the transportation of said Doris Schornack, and it would be mere conjecture on the part of this court were we to decide that the respondent school districts did or did not exceed the authority granted them when they transported the said Doris Schornack as a pupil of the Groton Independent School District.

It is sufficient to state, that if the respondent school districts did not exceed the authority granted them, then they were performing a governmental function as an agent of the state, and in the absence of a statute imposing liability for negligence, they are not liable for negligence in the performance of such governmental function. . . . On the other hand, if the respondent school districts did exceed the authority granted them, then the acts of the school district officers in so exceeding their authority were ultra vires, and the districts cannot be held

liable for negligence in the performance of such acts which were ultr
vires and beyond the officers' scope of authority. . . .

The order sustaining the demurrer is affirmed.

Guides for Class Discussion

1. On what ground did the court make its decision?
2. Compare this case with *Tipton* v. *Willey, infra.*
3. Are you in agreement with this decision? Give reasons.

25. *"The principle of nonliability in the preformance of a govern
mental function does not, however, apply to a bus driver . .
[who] will be held personally liable for injuries to pupils growing
out of his own negligence"* (p. 6).

Tipton v. Willey,
47 Ohio App. 236, 191 N.E. 804 (1934)
(Decided by the Court of Appeals of Ohio, Gallia County)

[This was an action brought against a bus driver to recover
damages for personal injuries received by a six-year-old child when
he stepped off a school bus into a dangerous lane of traffic. Defendant demurred, and the lower court sustained the demurrer.
The higher court reversed the judgment of the lower court.]

Mauck, J.

. . . .

The defendant in this case, however, occupies a different relation to
the plaintiff than does the common carrier to its passenger. In this latter
relation the passenger by his voluntary and deliberate act engages the
services of the carrier, and is at liberty, of course, not to do so. In the
case at bar the plaintiff had no such election. His attendance at school
was compulsory and we may assume that the only practical means of
compliance with the law was to avail himself of the transportation
facilities afforded by the public authorities. As a child, he had the natural right to parental control and protection while at home. While
going to and from school and while there, he had the right to some

control and protection. It is true that for reasons of public policy the board of education as a quasi corporation is not charged with liability for failing to furnish him with needed care, but it is nevertheless the child's natural right. There is no reason, however, why the immunity enjoyed by the board of education for its negligent care of the pupil should attach to the defendant, who, as a private individual, undertakes for hire to safely transport the child to the school grounds. It is not questioned that he may be liable for his negligence, the only question being whether he was negligent.

. . . .

The judgment of the court of common pleas is reversed and the cause is remanded with directions that the demurrer be overruled and further proceedings had according to law.

Judgment reversed.

Guides for Class Discussion

1. Compare the decision in this case with *Schornack* v. *School District, supra.*
2. Do you think it is fair to hold the bus driver liable and not hold the school district liable? Give reasons.
3. See *Burnett* v. *Allen, infra.*

26. *"A bus driver will be held to be negligent unless he exercised the degree of care any reasonably prudent person would have exercised"* (p. 6).

Burnett v. Allen,
114 Fla. 489, 154 So. 515 (1934)
(Decided by the Supreme Court of Florida)

[This case originated as an action for damages against a bus driver for injuries received by a pupil being transported, and resulting from the alleged negligence of the driver. The lower court held in favor of the driver, and the plaintiff appealed. The higher court reversed the decision of the lower court and remanded the case. The question before the court was really the question of negligence.]

Buford, Justice.

. . . .

By assuming to perform the contract, alleged in the declaration, the defendant, by necessary implication, assumed to perform every act, reasonably necessary for the safety of the children intrusted to his care while in transportation, which would include the operation of safely receiving the children into the bus and in superintending and directing their safe exit from the bus and their safe departure from the bus.

The bus driver who contracts to furnish transportation and to transport school children from places at or near their residences to public free school becomes a special contractor for hire, and his contract of employment with the Board of Public Instruction becomes a contract with him made by the Board of Public Instruction for the use and benefit of each and every of those persons who are to be transported by him under the contract. As the contract contemplated the transportation of children who are incompetent to be charged with the assumption of risk because of their tender years and inexperience, it likewise contemplates, and by implication at least binds, the person contracting to furnish and conduct the means of transportation to use every reasonable precaution and care for the safety of such children and to prevent any harm or damage coming to them, either in approaching the bus, or while riding in the bus or when alighting from and leaving the immediate proximity of the bus at the completion of their journey, or at any time during the journey. Whether a person contracting and performing such a contract has used all such reasonable care and caution is a question for the determination of a jury in each case.

It may be that there is some conflict in authorities throughout the country as to the liability of a contracting school bus driver in cases of this character, but we think the weight of authority sustains the above enunciation.

Guides for Class Discussion

1. Compare this case with *Tipton* v. *Willey, supra.*
2. What did the court have to say regarding the degree of care required of bus drivers in order for them to avoid liability for negligence?
3. What implications does this decision have for school administrations?

27. *"It has been held that, since a school board is not liable for injuries to pupils while being transported, it does not have the implied authority to carry insurance to protect itself against the negligence of its employees"* (p. 6).

BOARD OF EDUCATION v. COMMERCIAL CASUALITY INS. CO.,

116 W. Va. 503, 182 S.E. 87 (1935)

(Decided by the Supreme Court of Appeals of West Virginia)

[When a county board of education succeeded a district board of education, the county board brought an action against defendant for the premiums paid by the district board on certain public liability and property damage insurance. On the ground that the district had no authority to carry the insurance, the county board attempted to get a refund on the premium paid by the district board. The lower court held in favor of the plaintiff, and the defendant appealed. The higher court affirmed the judgment of the lower court. Because there was no statute authorizing the district to carry liability insurance, the court found it necessary to rule on the question of whether the district had the implied authority so to do.]

MAXWELL, Judge.

. . . .

Under the code of 1931, a district board of education was vested with "general control and management of all the schools and the school interests of its district. . . ." Further, a board had authority "to provide at public expense for the transportation of pupils to and from such consolidated schools, or other schools where transportation of pupils may be necessary." Code, 18-5-13. Can it be reasonably said that the said statute, by implication, created the right in a district board to purchase indemnity insurance by reason of its operation of school buses?

Because it is a public agency, an arm of the state, a school board is not liable for damages for personal injury, even though such injury may arise from neglect or nonfeasance. . . . Nor can a board of education by the acquisition of indemnity insurance, or otherwise, change its status as a govermental agency. . . .

We are of opinion that under the law as it stood in 1932, when this insurance was purchased, there was no implied authority in a district board to procure insurance to facilitate the enforcement of bus drivers' liability. Since the date of the arising of this controversy, the statute has been enlarged. At present, a county board of education may "provide at public expense for insurance against the negligence of drivers of school buses operated by the board." Acts 1935, c. 60, amending Code, 18-5-13. It seems evident that the passage of this Act was in pursuance of legislative recognition that no such authority theretofore existed, and was not a mere crystallization of an existing authority arising from implication of law.

Guides for Class Discussion

1. Are you in agreement with the court's thinking on this question? Give reasons.
2. See *Schornack* v. *School District, supra.*
3. See also *Wallace* v. *Laurel County Board of Education, infra.*
4. If the board cannot carry insurance, what can it do to protect itself and the district?

28. *"Statutory authority to carry insurance does not affect the governmental immunity of a school board. . ." (p. 6).*

WALLACE v. LAUREL COUNTY BOARD OF EDUCATION,
287 Ky. 454, 153 S.W. (2d) 915 (1941)
(Decided by the Court of Appeals of Kentucky)

[When an eleven-year-old child, a passenger in a school bus operated by the school district, was killed, as a result of the alleged negligence of the driver, as he alighted from the bus, an action was brought against the district for damages. The board demurred, on the ground that it was performing a governmental function in transporting pupils and so was not liable. The lower court sustained the demurrer. In an amended petition, plaintiff contended that, as the board was at all times protected from liability by an insurance policy and any judgment which might be obtained against it would be satisfied by the insurance company, the district should be held liable. The district demurred to the amended petition, and the court again sustained the demurrer. The higher court agreed with the decision of the lower court.]

Sims, Commissioner.

. . . .

The fact that §§ 4399-20a and 4399-20b, Baldwin's 1941 Supplement, allow the Board to carry liability insurance against the negligence of drivers of school buses owned by the Board or operated under contract by it does not make the Board liable for the torts of its agents or employees. Williams' Adm'x v. Church Home for Females and Infirmary for Sick, 223 Ky. 355, 3 S.W. 2d 753, 62 A.L.R. 721. We have no statute imposing liability upon the Board on account of negligence by it or any of its employees in transporting children to and from school.

It is argued by appellant that § 4399-18 creating the Board as a body corporate with power "to sue and to be sued" makes it liable for tort, citing Bank of Hopkinsville v. Western Kentucky Asylum for Insane, 108 Ky. 357. It was held the bank had a cause of action against the Asylum to prevent the latter from diverting water from a stream so as to interfere with the operation of the former's mill. That opinion is rested on Herr v. Central Ky. Lunatic Asylum, 97 Ky. 458, 30 S.W. 971 . . ., wherein it was held that an injunction would lie against the Asylum to prevent it from damming and polluting the creek to the damage of lower riparian owner. It was pointed out in Board of Park Com'rs v. Prinz, 127 Ky. 460, 105 S.W. 948, that in the Bank and Herr cases there was what amounted to a taking of property within the meaning of § 242 of the Kentucky Constitution, and the right given by the statute to sue an arm of the state, such as an asylum, permitted suit against it on contracts; or to protect one's property; but such authority to sue did not embrace an action for tort committed by any of its officers or agents in the performance of a public duty. The rule enunciated in the Prinz case has been followed in an unbroken line of cases down to the present date. . . . Courts of other jurisdictions hold that the words "to sue and be sued" in the legislative acts creating Boards of Education do not authorize an action for negligence, but have reference to suits respecting matters within the scope of the duties of the Board. . . .

. . . .

We follow the almost universal rule that a school district or a school board, in the absence of a statute imposing it, is not subject to liability for injuries to pupils of public schools received in connection with their attendance thereat, since school districts or boards of education act as agents of the state in maintaining schools and perform a public or governmental duty, nolens volens, imposed upon them by law for the benefit of the public, and for the performance of which they receive no profit or advantage.

The Judge of the Laurel Circuit Court correctly sustained a demurrer to plaintiff's petition and his judgment in dismissing the petition an amended is affirmed.

Guides for Class Discussion

1. Compare this case with *Schornack* v. *School District, supra.*
2. Do you think this decision is equitable? Give reasons.

29. "*The ultra vires act of a school board in carrying liability insurance will not . . . excuse an insurance company from paying the amount stipulated in its insurance contract, so it has been held*" (p. 6).

THOMAS V. BROADLANDS COMMUNITY CONSOLIDATED SCHOOL DISTRICT,

348 Ill. App. 567, 109 N.E. (2d) 636 (1952)
(Decided by the Appellate Court of Illinois, Third District)

[This was an action to recover damages for injuries caused by the alleged negligence of the school district. Defendant moved to dismiss the complaint, and the lower court sustained the motion. On appeal, the higher court held that where the plaintiff, a student, was injured on the playground of the defendant district and the district carried liability insurance, the plaintiff could collect up to the amount of the policy's coverage from the district upon proof of negligence.]

O'CONNOR, Justice.

.   .   .   .

Does the liability insurance in force in behalf of the School District remove its immunity either totally or pro tanto? The answer to that question involves not only an analysis of decisions of this state, but also a research into the bases of the doctrine of governmental immunity.

.   .   .   .

. . . The only justifiable reason for the immunity of quasi-municipal corporations from suit for tort is the sound and unobjectionable one that it is the public policy to protect public funds and public property, to prevent the diversion of tax moneys, in this case school funds, to the payment of damage claims. There is no justification or reason for absolute immunity if the public funds are protected. Their protection has been the real and historical reason for the absolute immunity both elsewhere and in Illinois accorded quasi-municipal corporations, and similarly, municipal corporations in the exercise of a governmental function. Liability insurance, to the extent that it protects the public funds, removes the reason for, and thus the immunity to, suit. . . . If the public funds are protected by liability insurance, the justification and reason for the rule of immunity are removed.

Defendant, however, contends that there is no statutory authorization in Illinois for the carrying of an insurance policy by a School District which could result in the waiver of governmental immunity in such a situation. In effect defendant seeks to assert its own illegal act in procuring the insurance as a defense. We need not decide the question of waiver because immunity from tort liability of a quasi-municipal corporation is required or justified by the need for the protection of the public funds, and when liability insurance is available to so protect the public funds, the reason for the rule of immunity vanishes to the extent of the available insurance.

For the reasons stated the judgment of the trial court is reversed and the case is remanded.

Reversed and remanded.

Guides for Class Discussion

1. Do you agree with this decision?
2. Do you think this court would apply the same principle to a case involving injury resulting from transportation as it did to the injury here which grew out of negligence on the playground?
3. Compare this case with *Wallace* v. *Laurel County Board of Education, supra*. Which do you think represents the best law?

30. "*. . . school boards have the authority to make and enforce any reasonable rules governing the conduct of pupils. . . . In determining the reasonableness of a rule, a court will not substitute its own discretion for that of the board. . . .*" (p. 7).

STATE v. MARION COUNTY BOARD OF EDUCATION,
202 Tenn. 29, 302 S.W. (2d) 57 (1957)
(Decided by the Supreme Court of Tennessee)

[This was an action in mandamus to compel a county board of education to restore to enrollment a high-school student who was expelled for the remainder of the term during which she married. Because of a rash of marriages among high-school students, the board had enacted a rule providing that any student who married during the school term would be " 'expelled . . . for the remainder of the current term.' " In February of 1957 the young lady in question married. She was 18 years of age and was a senior in high school. Her scholastic attainments had been consistently high, and she anticipated graduating at the end of the term. When the board expelled her, her father-in-law brought this action, contending that "the rule is so unrelated to the interest of the school or its affairs as to amount to an abuse of discretion by the respondent Board of Education." The lower court refused to grant the writ and, on appeal, its action was affirmed.]

TOMLINSON, Justice.

.   .   .   .

If the representations made to the County Board of Education by every high school principal in Marion County as to their respective observations and experiences on this subject is at all accurate, then married students, and by virtue of the psychological effect thereof, for a few months immediately following marriage, have a detrimental influence upon fellow students, hence, a detrimental effect upon the progress and efficiency of the school. Therefore, if these principals know whereof they speak, the attendance during such period of such married students in the schools is within the bounds of reasonable regulation by the Board.

.   .   .   .

It is to be gathered from the statement of these teachers that some regulation is necessary. A milder one than that adopted by this resolution is not suggested. Nor does one occur to this Court. Based on this

ine of reasoning the conclusion must be that the regulation has a rea-
onable bearing on the progress and efficiency of these schools.

Boards of Education, rather than Courts, are charged with the important and difficult duty of operating the public schools. So, it is not
a question of whether this or that individual judge or court considers
a given regulation adopted by the Board as expedient. The Court's duty,
regardless of its personal views, is to uphold the Board's regulation unless it is generally viewed as being arbitrary and unreasonable. Any
other policy would result in confusion detrimental to the progress and
efficiency of our public school system.

.   .   .   .

The extreme to which a Court will go sometimes to carry out the
wholesome policy of not interfering with the acts of Boards of Education, unless clearly arbitrary and unreasonable, is reflected in the case
of Pugsley v. Sellmeyer, 158 Ark. 247, 250 S.W. 538, 30 A.L.R. 1212.
The regulation there forbade girl students from the use of cosmetics.
This rule was upheld by the majority opinion of that Court, and the
eighteen year old girl deprived of the privilege of attending school because she insisted upon putting face powder on her face. Maybe it
should be observed that this was back in 1923.

The decree of the Chancellor will be affirmed with costs adjudged
against the relator and his sureties.

Guides for Class Discussion

1. Compare this case with *Kissick* v. *Garland Independent School
   District, infra.*
2. In the absence of the rule in question, do you think the court
   could have expelled the girl? Give reasons.

31. "A board may enforce any reasonable rule with respect to the time and age at which beginning pupils may enter school" (p. 7).

STATE V. SCHOOL DISTRICT NO. 1 OF FERGUS COUNTY,
136 Mont. 453, 348 P. (2d) 797 (1960)
(Decided by the Supreme Court of Montana)

[When a child, who became six years of age three days after the final date specified in a board rule for eligibility to enrollment in the first grade, was, as a result, denied admission, this action was brought to compel the board to admit him. Plaintiff questioned the legality of the rule because of a statute that required the maintenance of schools open to all children between the ages of six and twenty-one. The lower court ruled he must be admitted and the district appealed. The higher court set aside the writ granted by the lower court.]

CASTLES, Justice.

. . . .

The merits of the matter present this question: Does a school board have power under our Constitution and statutes to set an arbitrary date, after the beginning of a school term, after which a child who reaches his sixth birthday may not be admitted for that particular term?

. . . .

It is petitioner's contention, and that of the district court, that the wording "school . . . shall be open to all children . . . between the age of six and twenty-one years" must be given a literal interpretation, "all" being all inclusive and mandatory.

. . . .

But, we shall examine the wording of the Constitution and statutes to determine what was meant by the framers of the Constitution. In other words, what does the term "all" mean? Should it be taken in its universal and omnibus sense, that is, literally all? Or rather, was it meant to be limited and qualified to conform to good reason to carry out the other purposes of the Constitution such as to have a general, uniform and thorough system of public schools?

. . . .

We feel that neither the framers of the Constitution nor the Legislature could have intended that Article XI, section 7, and section 75-2004

ompel local school districts to admit children immediately upon attain-
ıg the age of six years at any time. A reasonable interpretation of
hese provisions, in connection with the other provisions requiring a
horough education is that a child must be allowed to enter the first
rade sometime during his seventh year after reaching his sixth birth-
ay. . . .

. . . Each local school district has the power to admit children into
he first grade who are not six years of age. This is discretionary and
hould be decided so that the best interests of the school and child
ıay be subserved to obtain a general, uniform and thorough system of
ublic, free, common schools. Each school district may establish a
"cut-off" date governing entry into the first grade. . . . By the establish-
nent of this date, the school districts may refuse admission to a child
vho becomes six after the "cut-off" date, yet during the school year. . . .

The rule establishing the "cut-off" date must be reasonable and not
vork an undue hardship on the children to whom it applies. While the
ule adopted by the School Board in the instant case is not a model
ule for any school district to adopt, in our view, as the Board in-
erpreted it, it is a reasonable rule. It provides an initial "cut-off" date
of October 31st, beyond which parents are discouraged from entering
heir children in the first grade. Those children who become six between
Dctober 31st and November 15th may be admitted at the parent's
request, providing that a test be administered to those children whose
oirthdays fall between November 1st and November 15th. By this
rule, a child may be admitted to the first grade up to two and one-half
months after the start of the normal school year. This is a reasonable
length of time, in our view, to hold the school open for enrollment of
children entering the first grade. While it is true that this rule embodies
only arbitrary dates, we consider this to be a sufficiently reasonable rule
under the circumstances.

Guides for Class Discussion

1. Does this decision promote the best interests of both the
   school and the child?
2. How far can a board go in enacting rules of the type mentioned
   here without being unreasonable?

32. *"Rules regulating the dress of pupils have been held to b*
reasonable" (p. 7).

PUGSLEY v. SELLMEYER,

158 Ark. 247, 250 S.W. 538 (1923)
(Decided by the Supreme Court of Arkansas)

[This was an action brought by a student who had been disci
plined for infringing a board rule that stated: "The wearing o
transparent hosiery, low-necked dresses or any style of clothing
tending toward immodesty in dress, or the use of face paint o
cosmetics, is prohibited." Primarily she was accused of using
talcum powder. When she refused to submit to, or obey the rule
she was denied admission. She brought this action to be reinstated
The lower court ruled against her, and the higher court affirmed
its decision.]

SMITH, J. . . .

. . . .

Was the rule in question a reasonable one, and did the directors
have the right to make and enforce it? We answer this question in the
affirmative. . . .

. . . .

The question . . . is not whether we approve this rule as one we
would have made as directors of the district, nor are we required to
find whether it was essential to the maintenance of discipline. On the
contrary, we must uphold the rule unless we find that the directors have
clearly abused their discretion, and that the rule is not one reasonably
calculated to effect the purpose intended, that is, of promoting discipline
in the school; and we do not so find.

. . . .

Courts have other and more important functions to perform than
that of hearing the complaints of disaffected pupils of the public schools
against rules and regulations promulgated by the school boards for the
government of the schools. The courts have this right of review, for
the reasonableness of such rule is a judicial question, and the courts
will not refuse to perform their functions in determining the reasonableness of such rules, when the question is presented. But, in doing so, it
will be kept in mind that the directors are elected by the patrons of
the schools over which they preside, and the election occurs annually.
These directors are in close and intimate touch with the affairs of

heir respective districts, and know the conditions with which they
have to deal. . . .

In the discharge of the duty here imposed upon us it is proper for
s to consider whether the rule involves any element of oppression or
humiliation to the pupil, and what consumption of time or expenditure
f money is required to comply with it. It does not appear unreasonable
in any of these respects. Upon the contrary, we have a rule which im-
oses no affirmative duty, and no showing was made, or attempted, that
he talcum powder possessed any medicinal properties, or was used
therwise than as a cosmetic.

We are unwilling to say, as a matter of law, that a local condition
might not exist which would make a rule of this character desirable in
id of the discipline of the school, and we therefore decline to annul it,
or we will not annul a rule of the kind unless a valid reason for doing
o is made to appear; whereas, to uphold it, we are not required to
ind a valid reason for its promulgation.

Guides for Class Discussion

1. What are the criteria for what is reasonable?
2. Do you think a court today would hold as this court did in
   1923? Why or why not?
3. What authority does the court have with respect to school-
   board rules?

33. "*A board may make the taking of a physical examination a
condition of school attendance, and it may exclude from school
pupils whose presence would jeopardize the health of other pupils*"
(p. 7).

STREICH v. BOARD OF EDUCATION,

34 S.D. 169, 147 N.W. 779 (1914)
(Decided by the Supreme Court of South Dakota)

[The question before the court in this case was the right of a
school board to require children seeking admission to school to
furnish evidence of having taken a physical examination. In this
case a parent with two children of school age refused to permit
them to take a physical examination, and the children were denied

admission. The lower court upheld the action of the board, and the higher court affirmed the action of the lower court.]

WHITING, J. . . .

. . . .

Need a child suffer any indignity or a violation of any sacred right by submitting to such physical examination as would be necessary in order that a physician might fill out the report called for? Appellant did not prove, nor do we find anything in the report requiring, that there need be any exposure of the person of the child or any manipulation of its body such as would shock the sensibilities of the most refined person. Here, again, we must not overlook the person who makes the examination; the conventionalities of our time recognize the absolute propriety of submitting one's body to the examination of a physician whenever such examination is made for the purpose of gaining information concerning one's physical condition. The established customs—the conventionalities of the time—are matters to be considered in determining the reasonableness of a particular action; therefore a thing may be reasonable, though it conflicts with the individual views of the few if it conforms to that of the many. Such an examination as the report calls for could not subject a child to anything not in perfect harmony with the conventions of to-day, could not subject it to indignity, and would be reasonable.

. . . .

Appellant's brief suggests that the requiring of the physical examination of appellant's child against appellant's wishes is "an invasion of the rights of citizens under the Constitution and laws of the land, and the higher right of the freedom of his mental determination of that which to him constitutes the most sacred right, and to him it may be a part of his worship of Deity." In these last words we might conclude there was to be found the real foundation of appellant's opposition to the rule which he is seeking to have set aside, were it not for the fact that his counsel, upon the oral argument of this cause, repeatedly assured this court that the question before us was in no sense a religious question, but one entirely separate and distinct from any one's religious belief. We agree fully with counsel as certainly the school boards of our land, in making rules for the control of our public schools, should not base the same upon the tenets of any particular religious sect or sects.

Repeating again that the reasonableness of any rule involving the exercise of police power must depend upon the particular circumstances surrounding the making of the rule, and that, for that reason, each case must stand by itself, we have no hesitancy in holding that the requiring of the report in question was, under all the surrounding conditions, reasonable.

The judgment appealed from is affirmed.

Guides for Class Discussion

1. Compare the decision in this case with that in *Martin* v. *Craig, supra.*
2. Assuming that back of the opposition to this rule were religious objections, do you think the court acted properly? Give reasons.

34. "*Statutes which authorize or require vaccination against smallpox or immunization against diphtheria as a prerequisite of school attendance have been held to be constitutional, as have also school-board regulations to this effect adopted under permissive statutes*" (p. 7).

BOARD OF EDUCATION V. MAAS,

56 N. J. S. 245, 152 A. (2d) 394 (1959)
(Decided by the Superior Court of New Jersey, Appellate Division)

[This case was an appeal from a decision of a lower court in favor of plaintiff board of education. The judgment was the culmination of litigation involving several claims arising out of defendant's attempts to gain admission to the Mountain Lakes (N.J.) public schools of three children temporarily residing in this country. Under authority of a statute permitting it to do so, the board had adopted a regulation requiring pupils to be vaccinated against smallpox and immunized against diphtheria as a prerequisite to admission. Defendant, a Christian Scientist, sponsored the admission to the United States of three Greek children for a limited stay. When she attempted to enroll them in school without complying with the regulation the board refused to accept them. Nevertheless, she brought them to school and left them there. After this occurred several times, the board obtained an injunction against her to compel her to refrain from so doing. From this action she appealed. Among other things, she contended the resolution requiring vaccination and immunization was unconstitutional. The court held otherwise.]

GOLDMANN, S. J. A. D.

.   .   .   .

The core question on this appeal is defendant's contention that the compulsory vaccination and immunization regulation adopted by the board deprived her of due process and religious freedom, within the contemplation of the United States Constitution, Amendments I or XIV and the New Jersey Constitution (1947), Art. I, pars. 3 and 5.

A requirement that a child must be vaccinated and immunized before it can attend the local public schools violates neither due process nor (as defendant tangentially suggests) the equal protection clause of the Constitution. The rationale of this rule is rooted in traditional concepts recognizing the authority of a local board, acting under a legislative grant of power, to promote the community health, safety and welfare. The fact that there may be differences of opinion as to the necessity or efficacy of vaccination or immunization does not deprive the State of the power to enact legislation requiring compulsory vaccination or immunization, or the local board from acting pursuant to such a power. . . .

.   .   .   .

Defendant points out that 18 states have no compulsory vaccination laws and that many New Jersey municipalities do not require vaccination or immunization. This in no way affects the issue before us; the Legislature has chosen to act within the broad field of state police power, and the municipality has adopted a policy pursuant to legislative authority granted. Their right to do so may not be challenged at this late date.

Defendant also argues that compulsory vaccination and immunization is not called for in Mountain Lakes because there has been no case of smallpox or diphtheria for almost a decade. The absence of an existing emergency does not warrant a denial to the regulative agency of the exercise of preventive means. A local board of education need not await an epidemic, or even a single sickness or death, before it decides upon action to protect the public. To hold otherwise would be to destroy prevention as a means of combatting the spread of disease. . . .

Nor did the local regulation abridge religious freedom within the meaning of the Federal and State Constitutions. In considering the compulsory vaccination of school children under R.S. 18:14-52, N.J. S.A. adopted by the local board of education in the Sadlock case, the court rejected the precise religious issue here raised by defendant, when it said: "So, too, with respect to the guaranty of religious liberty, the constitutional guaranty of religious freedom was not intended to prohibit legislation with respect to the general public welfare."

Guides for Class Discussion

1. Compare this decision with *Bissell* v. *Davison, supra.*
2. Compare this decision with *Anderson* v. *State, infra.*

3. Do you think the court would have held as it did if the board regulation had required immunization from poliomyelitis? Give reasons.

35. *"In the absence of statutory authority, as a general rule, the courts will not enforce a rule requiring vaccination against small-pox as a condition of school attendance unless there is an actual or threatened epidemic of smallpox in the community"* (p. 7).

MATHEWS V. BOARD OF EDUCATION,
127 Mich. 530, 86 N.W. 1036 (1901)
(Decided by the Supreme Court of Michigan)

[This was an action in mandamus brought by a parent to compel the defendant board to allow plaintiff's children to attend school without vaccination. In this case the board, in the absence of any statute authorizing or permitting it to do so, had enacted a rule requiring that all children be vaccinated. Plaintiff, a Christian Scientist, conscientiously objected. The board justified its action on the ground that, while there had been no smallpox in the City of Kalamazoo or in the school district, the disease had been and continued to be prevalent in several parts of the United States, including other areas in Michigan. The lower court granted the writ, and the higher court affirmed the decision of the lower court. In so doing the court took the position that there was no epidemic in the immediate area and in the absence of such the board did not have the authority to enact the rule it did.]

MOORE, J. . . .

. . . .

. . . It is said that the board does not undertake to compel vaccination, but it simply says that until the child is vaccinated it cannot attend school. We have already shown that it is made by law the duty of the child to attend school, and of the parent to send him; and, as long as the broad rule adopted by the board exists, the child must be vaccinated, or it and its parents must be lawbreakers. If the rule was that during the prevalence of the smallpox in Kalamazoo the child could not attend school unless vaccinated, a very different result would be reached. These epidemics never last very long, and the parent and child might well say, if they desired, that they would absent themselves from school during the epidemic; and this could be done without their being lawbreakers. . . . As the police power imposes restrictions and burdens upon the natural and private rights of individuals, it necessarily depends upon the law for its support, and, although of comprehensive and far-reaching character, it is subject to constitutional restrictions; and, in general, it is the province of the lawmaking power to determine in what cases or upon what conditions this power may be exercised. As applied to the present case, the relator had a right secured by statutory enactment, to have his children continue to attend the city schools in which they were respectively enrolled as pupils; and they, too, had a right to so attend such schools. Whether it be called a "right" or "privilege" cannot be important, for in either view it was secured to the relator, and to his children as well, by the positive provisions of law, and was to be enjoyed upon such terms and under such conditions and restrictions as the lawmaking power, within constitutional limits, might impose. There is no statute in this state authorizing compulsory vaccination, nor any statute which requires vaccination as one of the conditions of the right or privilege of attending the public schools; and, in the absence of any such statute, we think it cannot be maintained that the rule relied upon is a valid exercise of the rightful powers of the state board of health. . . . It is not a question as to what the legislature might do, under the police power, about requiring vaccination as a prerequisite to attending school; nor is it a question of whether the legislature could confer this power upon the school board. The board of education is a creature of the statute. It possesses only such powers as the statute gives it. The legislature has said who may and should attend the public schools. It has nowhere undertaken to confer the power upon the school board to change these conditions by passing a general, continuing rule excluding children from the public schools until they comply with conditions not imposed upon them by the legislative branch of the government. In what I have said I do not mean to intimate that during the prevalence of diphtheria or smallpox, or any other epidemic or contagious disease, in a school district, the board may not, under its general powers, temporarily close the schools, or temporarily say who shall be excluded from the schools until the epidemic has passed; but what I do say is that the legislature has not undertaken to give them the power, when no epidemic of contagious disease exists or is imminent in the district, to pass a general, continuing rule which would have the effect of a general law excluding all pupils who will not submit to vaccination. I think the learned judge was right in saying the school board exceeded its power. The order of the court below is affirmed.

Guides for Class Discussion

1. Compare this case with *Board of Education* v. *Maas, supra.* Differentiate between the reasoning of the courts in these two cases.
2. Do you agree with the court's thinking? Give reasons.
3. Do you think a court today would hold as did the court here? Why or why not?

36. *"A pupil cannot defeat the operation of a rule or law requiring vaccination on the ground that it violates his freedom of conscience"* (p. 7).

ANDERSON V. STATE,
84 Ga. App. 259, 65 S.E. (2d) 848 (1951)
(Decided by the Court of Appeals of Georgia)

[This was an action against certain parents for refusing to keep their children in school as required under the compulsory-education law. They had attempted to enroll the children, but the school refused to accept them, because they failed to comply with a board rule, authorized by statute, requiring children entering school to be immunized against smallpox, diphtheria, and typhoid, at least. The parents defended their actions on religious grounds. The lower court ruled against them, and the higher court upheld the actions of the lower court.]

TOWNSEND, Judge. . . .

. . . .

. . . The defendants contend that they are members of a religious sect which permits them to choose for themselves the application of the tenets of their sect; that they interpret their religious instruction to mean that they should not use medicinal aids; that this is a part of their religion and to deprive them of it is to deprive them of their freedom of worship; that they do not wish to deprive their children of an education but when forced to make a choice between depriving them of an education and allowing them to receive medical treatment they must choose the former. The ill effects of contagious disease, and its power to wipe out entire populations, is a matter of history. . . . The purpose of the legislature in passing the statute . . . [authorizing the board to enact the rule requiring immunization] was to prevent the spread of these diseases, not only for the protection of those actually immunized but for the protection of others with whom they might come in contact. The refusal of the defendants here to have their children vaccinated amounted to a transgression of the rights of others. . . .

Liberty of conscience is one thing. License to endanger the lives of others by practices contrary to statutes passed for the public safety and in reliance upon modern medical knowledge is another. The validity of the statute is not questioned, and the wisdom of the legislative enactment is not a matter for the decision either of this court or of any individual citizen. The opinion of the defendants that they should practice healing without the aid of medicine is not a legal justification for refusal to abide by the statutes of this state and regulations passed pursuant thereto, and for this reason freedom of worship was not an issue in the case. The failure of the court to charge on this subject was not error.

. . . .

Code Supp. § 32-2104 imposes upon parents of children between the ages of seven and sixteen years the duty of enrolling and sending such children to a public or private school. Code Supplement § 32-9914 fixes the penalty for noncompliance with this duty. As hereinbefore pointed out, Code and Supplement § 32-911 empowers the county boards of education to fix rules and regulations insuring the vaccination of such school children as a prerequisite to admission. These provisions of our statute law therefore impose upon the parents the duty of sending the children to school and upon the school authorities the duty of fixing the rules and regulations under which they shall attend. The defendants in this case sought to comply with their duty to send their children to school but at the same time usurp the prerogative of the school authorities, and also undertook to fix the rules under which they should attend. . . . Further, our statute specifically provides, not only that the child shall be enrolled, but kept in school for a minimum of 175 days or the full session thereof, subject to certain exceptions. Under these circumstances, the action of the parents in refusing to meet the prerequisites of attendance in public school constituted a violation of the statute and the court did not err in so charging.

The judgment of the trial court overruling the motion for a new trial as amended is without error.

Judgment affirmed.

Guides for Class Discussion

1. Compare this case with *Board of Education* v. *Maas, supra.*
2. Compare this case with *Commonwealth* v. *Renfrew, supra.*
3. Do you agree with the court's reasoning? Give reasons.
4. Do you feel that such statutes and rules as here considered violate the First or Fourteenth Amendments to the Constitution of the United States?

37. "*Statutes authorizing or requiring boards of education to expel pupils who belong to fraternities or secret societies have been held to be constitutional . . .*" (p. 7).

BRADFORD V. BOARD OF EDUCATION,

18 Cal. App. 19, 121 P. 929 (1912)

(Decided by the District Court of Appeal, First District, California)

[This was an action in mandamus to require a board of education to reinstate a pupil who had been suspended because, while enrolled as a pupil, she joined a Greek letter sorority existing in the school in violation of an act of the legislature. She argued the act was unconstitutional. The lower court denied the writ of mandamus and the higher court affirmed the decision of the lower court.]

KERRIGAN, J. . . .

.   .   .   .

In support of her contention that the act is void, appellant first claims that it contravenes section 21 of article 1 of the Constitution, providing, "Nor shall any citizen or class of citizens be granted privileges or immunities which upon the same terms shall not be granted to all citizens"; and also that part of section 25 of article 4 providing that the Legislature shall not pass local or special laws, "granting to any corporation, association or individual any special or exclusive right, privilege or immunity."

It is argued by counsel that this contravention of constitutional provisions arises because the act grants an immunity to certain pupils in the public schools of the state, viz., those in the normal schools, in tha only the elementary and secondary schools come within the provision of the act; that it grants a special privilege to such pupils by allowing them to join fraternities, sororities, and secret clubs while other student in the public schools are punished for doing the same thing. . . .

The question of the construction and application of said section 21 of article 1 has come before the Supreme Court of this state in many cases and among them quite recently in the case of Wheeler v. Herbert, 15: Cal. 233, 92 Pac. 357, where that court said (speaking through Mr Justice Shaw): "A law applying uniformly to all citizens of a particular class does not violate this section (Const. art. 1, § 21), if the class is one founded upon some natural, intrinsic or constitutional distinction differentiating its members from the general body from which the class is selected"—citing California cases.

.   .   .   .

Applying this construction to the act under consideration, it is quite apparent to us that the younger and more immature pupils of the public schools may quite properly form a class and be made the subject of this character of legislation. Normal schools and colleges are attended by students who are preparing for the serious affairs of life; and being older in years and with wider experience are better fortified to withstand any possible hurtful influence attendant upon membership in secret societies and clubs than the younger pupils attending elementary and secondary schools, who are less experienced and more impressionable.

We have no doubt that there is a sufficient difference between these last-mentioned schools and the normal to constitute a proper basis for classification, and that the statute applies equally to all of the particular class mentioned. . . .

We hold, therefore, that the act is general in its character and not special, and does not contravene the provisions of the Constitution referred to.

Guides for Class Discussion

1. See *Wilson* v. *Board of Education, infra.*
2. Do you think the court was correct in holding as it did? Give reasons.

38. *"Boards of education have the implied authority to limit the privileges of pupils who maintain membership in fraternities or secret societies"* (p. 7).

WILSON V. BOARD OF EDUCATION,
233 Ill. 464, 84 N.E. 697 (1908)
(Decided by the Supreme Court of Illinois)

[In this case certain students who were barred from participating in extra-curricular activities because of membership in a high school fraternity, in violation of a rule of the board of education of the City of Chicago, brought this action to enjoin the board from enforcing the rule. The lower court approved the rule, and the higher court affirmed the judgment of the lower court.]

MR. JUSTICE FARMER delivered the opinion of the court:

. . . .

Counsel for plaintiff in error does not question the power of the board of education to prescribe all reasonable rules necessary for the conduct and management of the public schools, but insists that the rule here involved was not a reasonable rule; that it was in violation of the natural rights of plaintiff in error and an unlawful discrimination against him, and that this is a question of law to be determined by the courts. It is not claimed nor averred in the bill that plaintiff in error was deprived, by the rule in question, from attendance at the school nor from taking his place in the classes to which he belonged and pursuing his studies and receiving instruction, the same as all other pupils in the school, in the course of studies taught therein. . . . The power of the board of education to control and manage the schools and to adopt rules and regulations necessary for that purpose is ample and full. The rules and by-laws necessary to a proper conduct and management of the schools are, and must necessarily be, left to the discretion of the board, and its acts will not be interfered with nor set aside by the courts unless there is a clear abuse of the power and discretion conferred. Acting reasonably within the powers conferred, it is the province of the board of education to determine what things are detrimental to the successful management, good order and discipline of the schools and the rules required to produce these conditions. It was the judgment of the superintendent of schools of the city of Chicago, as well as of the board of education, that membership in secret societies, known as Greek letter fraternities or sororities, was detrimental to the best interests of the schools. Whether this judgment was sound and well founded is not subject to review by the courts. . . .

. . . .

. . . The rule adopted by the board of education, and which is set out in full in the bill, shows upon its face that it was not the result of hasty and ill-considered action. At a previous meeting the board had instructed the superintendent of schools to investigate the effect of secret societies upon the schools, and upon his report that he had made the investigation, and upon his recommendation, the rule was adopted. Assuming, as we must, that the adoption of the rule was not an abuse of power or discretion conferred by law upon the board, courts cannot and should not, interfere with its enforcement. Pupils attending the schools may decide for themselves whether they prefer membership in the secret societies, with the disqualification from representing their schools in literary or athletic contests or other public capacities, or whether they prefer these latter privileges to membership in said societies. It is for the board of education, within the reasonable exercise of its power and discretion, to say what is best for the successful management and conduct of the schools, and not for the courts.

In our opinion the bill was properly dismissed, and the judgment of the Appellate Court is affirmed.

Judgment affirmed

Guides for Class Discussion

1. Compare the decision in this case with *Bradford* v. *Board of Education, supra.*

2. How do you think the court would have held had the board rule provided for suspension or expulsion of pupils who were members of fraternities, instead of simply barring them from extracurricular activities?

3. What is the limit of a board's authority in a case of this type?

39. "It has been held . . . that boards of education may deny to married pupils the right to participate in such extracurricular activities as football" (p. 7).

KISSICK V. GARLAND INDEPENDENT SCHOOL DISTRICT,
330 S.W. (2d) 708 (Tex.) (1959)
(Decided by the Court of Civil Appeals of Texas)

[This was an action by plaintiff to restrain the board from enforcing a resolution providing that "married students or previously married students be restricted wholly to classroom work; that they be barred from participating in athletics or other exhibitions, and they not be permitted to hold class offices or other positions of honor. Academic honors such as Valedictorian and Salutatorian are excepted." The plaintiff in this case was a letter man on the 1958 football team. In March of 1959, at the age of 16, he was married, and as a result of the board's rule was barred from further participation in athletic activities. Among other things, it was stated that he planned to continue football, in the hope he might eventually get an athletic scholarship in some college. The resolution was attacked as discriminatory, unreasonable, and unconstitutional. It was also contended that it was applied illegally—i.e., retroactively—in that it was not enacted by the board until after he married. The lower court upheld the legality of the rule, and the higher court affirmed its decision.]

YOUNG, Justice.

. . . .

With regard to authority of school trustees, it is uniformly held that "the courts will not interfere in such matters unless a clear abuse of power and discretion is made to appear." . . . We shall reserve a discussion of appellant's first point (the resolution as arbitrary, unreasonable, etc.) until later in this opinion.

Appellant asserts that such resolution is violative of public policy in that it penalizes persons because of marriage. Consistent with limitations and requirements of State Statutes, both civil and criminal, the point is overruled. Art. 4603, V.A.C.S., provides that "males under sixteen and females under fourteen years of age shall not marry." Art. 404, Vernon's Ann. Penal Code, makes it a criminal offense for the County Clerk to issue a marriage license to males under twenty-one or females under eighteen without consent of parents or guardian, or in lieu thereof the County Judge, under penalty of a $1,000 fine. Art. 4605, V.A.C.S., places similar restrictions on issuance of a marriage license to males under twenty-one and females under eighteen. And in the summer of 1959 our Legislature evidenced its concern over the problem of "teen-age" marriages by amending Art. 4605. Issuance of license to marry was prohibited to such underage applicants except "upon the consent and authority *expressly given* by the parent or guardian of such underage applicant *in the presence of the authority issuing such license*", . . . (emphasis ours); also requiring that application therefor be on file in the County Clerk's office for not less than three days prior thereto.

As appellant states, it is indeed the policy of the law to look with favor upon marriage and to seek in all lawful ways to uphold this most important of social institutions; every intendment being in favor of matrimony. . . . The principle however is referable to those of lawful age (male twenty-one, female eighteen). On the other hand, the legislative policy is otherwise insofar as an underage marriage is concerned; it being clearly manifest that by the cited statutes a public policy is announced unfavorable to and in outright discouragement of "underage applicants" for matrimony.

. . . .

We now recur to the first and controlling issue of law raised by appellant; of whether the resolution was "arbitrary, capricious, discriminatory, unreasonable and void". Undoubtedly it had a direct relationship to objectives sought to be accomplished by school authorities—that of discouraging the marriage of "teen-age" students. A similar problem was faced by the School in State ex rel. Thompson v. Marion County Board of Education, Tenn., 302 S.W. 2d 57, 58. There the Board had passed a resolution to the effect that any student who married during the school term should be automatically expelled "for the remainder of the current term". If the marriage took place during vacation, such student should not be allowed to attend school "during the term next succeeding". Under said order, the married student could resume attendance at any later full term. In upholding this regulation as not amounting to an abuse of discretion the Tennessee Supreme Court made the following observation, with which we agree: "Boards of Education, rather than Courts, are charged with the important and difficult duty of operating the public schools. So, it is not a question of whether this or that individual judge or court considers a given regulation adopted by the Board as expedient. The Court's duty, regardless of its personal views, is to uphold the Board's regulation unless it is generally viewed as being arbitrary and unreasonable. Any other policy would result in confusion detrimental to the progress and efficiency of our public school system."

All points of appeal upon consideration are overruled and judgment of the trial court affirmed.

Guides for Class Discussion

1. Do you agree with the court that the rule in question was a reasonable one?
2. Compare this case with *State* v. *Marion County Board of Education, supra.*
3. Do you think the court would have held as it did, had the board rule barred the married student from taking certain academic courses rather than engaging in an extra-curricular activity? Give reasons.

40. *"The state has the authority to require the pupils in its schools to take those studies that are essential for good citizenship" (p. 8).*

PEOPLE V. STANLEY,
81 Colo. 276, 255 P. 610 (1927)
(Decided by the Supreme Court of Colorado)

[This was an action in mandamus brought against a school board to compel it to revoke a rule requiring Bible reading as a portion of the morning exercises. The board demurred. The lower court upheld the demurrer, and the higher court modified the decision and affirmed the action of the lower court. While the question involved the right of the school district to require Bible reading, the court found it necessary to comment on the right of the board to require pupils to take studies that are essential to good citizenship.]

DENISON, J. . . .

. . . .

The state, for its own protection, may require children to be educated. This needs no citation.

Certain studies plainly essential to good citizenship must be taught. . . . And, as a corollary, such studies may be required of every child.

Liberty is more than freedom from imprisonment. The right to conduct a private school; the right of parents to have their children taught where, when, how, what, and by whom they may judge best, are among the liberties guaranteed by section 1 of the Fourteenth Amendment of the United States Constitution. . . .

.   .   .   .

Conversely, the teaching of what is immoral or inimical to the public welfare may be forbidden by the state, even though taught as a moral and religious duty; e.g., polygamy. . . .

It necessarily follows that, if parents can have their children taught what they please, they can refuse to have them taught what they think harmful, barring what must be taught; i.e., the essentials of good citizenship. What these are the board of education of each district, primarily, and the courts ultimately, must decide. So whether any study is immoral or inimical to the public welfare the board primarily and the courts ultimately must decide.

Guides for Class Discussion

1. In light of the court's comments, what studies are essential to good citizenship?
2. Compare the decision in this case with *Wulff* v. *Inhabitants of Wakefield, infra;* with *People ex rel. Ring* v. *Board of Education, infra;* with *Schempp* v. *Abington Township School District, infra;* and *Chamberlin* v. *Dade County Board of Public Instruction, infra.*

41. "*In the absence of statute authorizing a board of education to require that pupils pursue a particular subject, according to the weight of authority, a parent may make any reasonable selection of the studies his child will pursue from those offered by the school*" (p. 8).

STATE V. SCHOOL DISTRICT,
31 Neb. 552, 48 N.W. 393 (1891)
(Decided by the Supreme Court of Nebraska)

[This was an action brought by a parent to test his right to have his child excused from a class in grammar on the ground that "said study was not taught in said school as he had been instructed when he went to school." When the school expelled the child for refusing to study courses she was asked to take, this action was brought to have her reinstated. The question before the court was the right of the parent to select studies he wished his child to pursue. The lower court ordered the child reinstated, and the higher court affirmed the decision of the lower court.]

MAXWELL, J. . . .

. . . Under the power here given, the trustees may require the classification of the pupils with regard to the branches of study they are respectively pursuing, and with respect to proficiency in the same branches. They may also require prompt attendance, respectful deportment, and diligence in study. Such regulations are for the benefit of all, and tend to promote a common interest and the efficiency of the school. Neither has a parent any right to require that the interests of other children shall be sacrificed for the interest of his children. Therefore he cannot insist that his child or children shall be placed in a particular class when, by so doing, other pupils will be retarded in the advancement they would otherwise make; neither can he require that his children be taught branches different from those in the prescribed course of the school, or be allowed to use textbooks different from those required by the trustees; nor will he be allowed to adopt methods of study for his children which interfere with methods adopted by the trustees, because in order to secure efficiency in the school it is necessary that the different classes work in harmony and cooperate together. . . .

The testimony tends to show that Anna Sheibley is about 15 years of age; that she is pursuing studies outside of those taught in the school, which occupy a portion of her time. Now, who is to determine wha studies she shall pursue in school,—a teacher who has a mere tem porary interest in her welfare, or her father, who may reasonably b supposed to be desirous of pursuing such course as will best promot the happiness of his child? The father certainly possesses superior op portunities of knowing the physical and mental capabilities of his child It may be apparent that all the prescribed course of studies is more tha the strength of the child can undergo, or he may be desirous, as is fre quently the case, that his child while attending school should also tak lessons in music, painting, etc., from private teachers. This he has ; right to do. The right of the parent, therefore, to determine what studie his child shall pursue is paramount to that of the trustees or teacher Schools are provided by the public, in which prescribed branches are taught, which are free to all within the district between certain ages, but no pupil attending the school can be compelled to study any pre scribed branch against the protest of the parent that the child shall not study such branch, and any rule or regulation that requires the pupi to continue such studies is arbitrary and unreasonable. There is no good reason why the failure of one or more pupils to study one or more prescribed branches should result disastrously to the proper discipline, efficiency, and well-being of the school.

Guides for Class Discussion

1. Do you think a court today would accept this decision?
2. Would the court have ruled as it did if the subject in question had been made mandatory by the statute?
3. Compare the decision in this case with *Wulff* v. *Inhabitants of Wakefield, infra.*

2. "A school board has the right to prescribe the method of instruction in any particular subject" (p. 8).

WULFF V. INHABITANTS OF WAKEFIELD,
221 Mass. 427, 109 N.E. 358 (1915)
(Decided by the Supreme Judicial Court of Massachusetts. Middlesex)

[This was an action in damages brought by plaintiff, who was excluded from high school when the school authorities refused to change the method of teaching bookkeeping, as requested by plaintiff's parents, and the plaintiff refused to attend the bookkeeping class. The lower court ruled in favor of the defendant and the higher court affirmed the decision of the lower court.]

PIERCE, J. There was evidence tending to show that for some reason, presumably because of the burden of work, the teacher selected a pupil as an assistant to perform in his stead the purely mechanical work of comparing the answers to problems as worked out by pupils with the correct answers contained in a "key book." It happened that a certain problem submitted by the plaintiff to the assistant for examination was marked "wrong." The plaintiff worked upon it as best she could during a week and a half and then again submitted it to the assistant, who again declared it "wrong." She continued to work upon it for another week and a half, and then submitted the same result to the teacher, who went over it and called it correct. There was evidence that as a consequence of this error of the assistant the plaintiff "worried, was nervous, and lost her appetite and sleep. . . . She reported the incident to her mother and her stepfather, Mr. and Mrs. Kleeman." Kleeman protested against the manner of correcting the papers in turn to the teacher, the superintendent of schools, and to the principal of the high school.

.   .   .   .

The real and vital question is not whether the plaintiff was guilty of misconduct in refusing to attend her class, but whether a parent has the right to say a certain method of teaching any given course of study shall be pursued. The question answers itself. Were it otherwise, should several parents hold diverse opinions all must yield to one or confusion and failure inevitably follow. The determination of the procedure and the management and direction of pupils and studies in this commonwealth rests in the wise discretion and sound judgment of teachers and school committee, whose action in these respects is not subject to the supervision of this court. . . .

Guides for Class Discussion

1. Compare the decision in this case with that in *People* v
   Stanley, supra; and with *State* v. *School District, supra.*
2. Are you in agreement with this decision? Give reasons.

43. ". . . *a school board may enforce its reasonable rules and
regulations governing the conduct of pupils off the school grounds
and after school hours*" (p. 8).

JONES v. CODY,
132 Mich. 13, 92 N.W. 495 (1902)
(Decided by the Supreme Court of Michigan)

[This was an action for damages against a principal of a public
school who enforced a rule of the board of education requiring
pupils to go directly to their homes at the close of school. The
action was brought by the owner of a store near the school building, who claimed that as a result of the enforcement of this rule he
suffered a loss of trade. The lower court held in favor of the
defendant, and the higher court affirmed the decision of the lower
court. The main point of the case involved the authority of the
school board to make a rule governing the conduct of pupils off
the school grounds and out of school hours.]

GRANT, J. . . .

The rule and the method of enforcing it are reasonable, unless it be
the law that those in control of our public schools have no jurisdiction
over pupils outside the schoolhouse yard. It is not only the legal right,
but the moral duty, of the school authorities, to require children to go
directly from school to their homes. All parents who have a proper regard for the welfare of their children desire it. The state makes it compulsory upon parents to send their children to school, and punishes
them for failure to do so. The least that the state can in reason do is
to throw every safeguard possible around the children who in obedience
to the law are attending school. The dangers to which children are exposed upon the streets of cities are matters of common knowledge.

umanity and the welfare of the country demand that a most watchful
feguard should, so far as possible, accompany children, when required
r allowed to be on the streets. Parents have a right to understand
rat their children will be promptly sent home after school, and to
elieve that something untoward has happened when they do not return
r time. In no other way can parents and teachers act in harmony to
rotect children from bad influences, bad companionship, and bad
rorals. No trader or merchant has the constitutional right to have chil-
ren remain in his place of business, in order that they may spend
roney there, while they are on their way to and from school. The
berty of neither the children nor parent nor trader is at all unlawfully
estrained by this rule and its reasonable enforcement. The rule does
rot interfere with the right of the parent to send his child upon an
rrand, to a store or other reputable place, or to the home of a relative
r friend to visit. Neither does it restrict the authority of parents over
heir children. This action on the part of the school board of the city
rf Detroit and its teachers is fully sustained by the authorities. . . .

Guides for Class Discussion

1. By what line of reasoning did the court arrive at its decision?
2. On what ground do you think the board should have the
   authority to enact rules governing the conduct of pupils off
   of school property and out of school hours?
3. Is such a rule essential to good administration?

44. *"A board of education may discipline a pupil for misbehavior
wherever committed, provided it directly affects school discipline
and is calculated to impair the efficiency of the school"* (p. 8).

Douglas v. Campbell,
89 Ark. 254, 116 S.W. 211 (1909)
(Decided by the Supreme Court of Arkansas)

[This was an action in damages by a parent against a teacher
and the school board who had expelled plaintiff's son from school
for allegedly having been drunk and disorderly on the streets of
the town on Christmas day. The father contended the charge was
untrue and the defendants knew it to be so, but that even if

the charge was true the offense was not in violation of any rule
of the school, and that it did not occur in the school or near the
school grounds. Defendants demurred. The lower court upheld
the demurrer and the higher court affirmed the decision of the
lower court.]

Wood, J. . . .

· · · · · · · · · ·

But appellant does not state facts sufficient to show an unlawful sus
pension. Being drunk and disorderly in violation of the ordinance of the
town as charged was sufficient cause for the punishment inflicted. Sec
tion 7637, Kirby's Dig., expressly authorizes the directors of any school
district "at the instance of the teacher to suspend from the school any
pupil for gross immorality, refractory conduct, or insubordination.
Wholesome discipline is absolutely essential to the success of any school.
Large discretion is allowed the teacher and the board within the statute
in determining what course of conduct on the part of the pupils is
necessary for the good of the whole school. That is the prime con
sideration. Any conduct on the part of a pupil that tends to demoraliz
other pupils, and to interfere with the proper and successful manage
ment of the school—i.e., to impair the discipline—which the teacher
and the board shall consider necessary for the best interest of the school
may subject the offending one to the punishment prescribed by the above
statute. "Refractory conduct, or insubordination," and gross immorality
are incompatible with that good government in a school which is abso
lutely essential to its success. Hence these are expressly mentioned in
the statute as conduct justifying the somewhat severe punishment of
suspension. It will be presumed that the teacher and the board have
the best interest of the school at heart, and that they have acted in
good faith in exercising the authority with which the law has clothed
them. The burden is upon him who calls in question their conduct to
show that they have not been actuated by proper motives. But, if the
teacher and board should through malice, arbitrarily, and without reason suspend a pupil from school, the pupil would have his remedy as
we have before mentioned, and the parent also would have his remedy
if he has sustained any pecuniary injury by reason of such illegal suspension.

Guides for Class Discussion

1. Do you think the rule that a board may discipline students
   for misbehavior, wherever committed, is a sound rule? Give
   reasons.

2. Compare the decision in this case with *Jones* v. *Cody, supra.*

3. Is the board's authority to discipline students for misbehavior, wherever committed, unlimited? Explain.

45. *"In some states the courts have held that Bible reading is sectarian instruction and violative of state constitutional provisions prohibiting instruction of this kind"* (p. 8).

People ex rel. Ring v. Board of Education,
245 Ill. 334, 92 N.E. 251 (1910)
(Decided by the Supreme Court of Illinois)

[This was an action in mandamus to require a board to cease enforcing a rule requiring Bible reading, the singing of hymns, and the reciting of the Lord's Prayer as opening exercises in the public schools. It should be noted that there was no statute covering this subject. The complaint contended that the rule of the board was unconstitutional. The board demurred and the lower court dismissed the petition. The higher court reversed the decision of the lower court and remanded the case, with directions.]

Dunn, J. . . .

.   .   .   .

Is the reading of the Bible in the public schools sectarian instruction? Religion has reference to man's relation to divinity; to the moral obligation of reverence and worship, obedience and submission. It is defined by Webster as the recognition of God as an object of worship, love, and obedience; right feeling toward God, as rightly apprehended. It deals with the soul. . . .

.   .   .   .

The question for decision is one of constitutional power. The Bible is not mentioned in our state Constitution. It was mentioned in the convention which framed the Constitution when it was sought to add to section 3 of article 8, a provision prohibiting the exclusion of the Bible from the public schools, but the amendment proposed was not adopted. . . .

Christianity is a religion. The Catholic Church and the various Protestant churches are sects of that religion. These two versions of the

Scriptures are the bases of the religion of the respective sects. Protestants will not accept the Douay Bible as representing the inspired word of God. As to them, it is a sectarian book containing errors and matter which is not entitled to their respect as a part of the Scriptures. It is consistent with the Catholic faith but not the Protestant. Conversely, Catholics will not accept King James' version. As to them, it is a sectarian book inconsistent in many particulars with their faith, teaching what they do not believe. The differences may seem to many so slight as to be immaterial, yet Protestants are not found to be more willing to have the Douay Bible read as a regular exercise in the schools to which they are required to send their children, than are Catholics to have the King James' version read in schools which their children must attend. . . .

The reading of the Bible in school is instruction. Religious instruction is the object of such reading, but whether it is so or not, religious instruction is accomplished by it. The Bible has its place in the school, if it is read there at all, as the living word of God, entitled to honor and reverence. Its words are entitled to be received as authoritative and final. The reading or hearing of such words cannot fail to impress deeply the pupils' minds. It is intended and ought to so impress them. . . .

We have been considering the case of the Protestant and the Catholic. Let us consider that of the Christian and the Jew. The Christian believes that Judaism was a temporary dispensation, and that Christ was the Messiah—the Savior of the world. The Jew denies that Christ was the Messiah and regards him as an impostor. Is it not the teaching of sectarian doctrine to his children to read to them daily from the New Testament, every chapter of which holds up Christ crucified as the Savior of men?

The Bible, in its entirety, is a sectarian book as to the Jew and every believer in any religion other than the Christian religion, and as to those who are heretical or who hold beliefs that are not regarded as orthodox. Whether it may be called sectarian or not, its use in the schools necessarily results in sectarian instruction. . . .

It is true that this is a Christian state. The great majority of its people adhere to the Christian religion. No doubt this is a Protestant state. The majority of its people adhere to one or another of the Protestant denominations. But the law knows no distinction between the Christian and the Pagan, the Protestant and the Catholic. All are citizens. Their civil rights are precisely equal. The law cannot see religious differences, because the Constitution has definitely and completely excluded religion from the law's contemplation in considering men's rights. There can be no distinction based on religion. The state is not, and under our Constitution cannot be, a teacher of religion. . . .

.   .   .   .

In our judgment the exercises mentioned in the petition constitute religious worship and the reading of the Bible in the school constitutes sectarian instruction. The demurrer to the amended petition should have been overruled.

The judgment is reversed, and the cause remanded to the circuit court, with directions to overrule the demurrer.

Reversed and remanded, with directions.

Guides for Class Discussion

1. Compare the decision in this case with *Chamberlin* v. *Dade County Board of Public Instruction, infra.*
2. Compare the decision in this case with *Schempp* v. *School District of Abington Township, infra.*
3. See *Commonwealth* v. *Renfrew, supra.*
4. Which of these cases represents the best law, in your opinion? Give reasons.
5. Do you think that the Bible is sectarian literature? Give reasons.

46. "*Most state courts, however, have ruled that statutes or board regulations permitting the reading of the Bible, the saying of The Lord's Prayer, or the singing of hymns are not in violation of prohibitions against religious or sectarian instruction*" (p. 8).

CHAMBERLIN V. DADE COUNTY BOARD OF PUBLIC INSTRUCTION,
143 So. (2d) 21 (Fla.) (1962)
(Decided by the Supreme Court of Florida)

[This decision was rendered when two cases involving similar issues and prayers for relief were consolidated. Both complaints sought to enjoin certain school practices that had religious over-tones and to have the court declare a Florida statute that required Bible reading daily, without sectarian comment, unconstitutional under the First and Fourteenth Amendments to the United States Constitution as well as under certain provisions of the Florida

Constitution. A school-board rule provided that children whose parents objected in writing, on religious grounds, should be excluded from Bible reading as well as other nonacademic activities. The lower court approved of the following practices: "The reading of the Bible; the distribution of sectarian literature to school children; the recitation of the Lord's Prayer, grace and other sectarian prayers; the singing of religious hymns; the display of religious symbols; [and] baccalaureate programs." It enjoined the following practices: "Sectarian comments by public school teachers; the use of school premises after school hours for Bible instruction; the exhibition of films with religious content and the religious observance in the public schools of Christmas, Easter and Hannukka holidays." In addition, it found there was no factual basis for allegations regarding a religious census and a religious test for teachers. Plaintiffs appealed and the higher court upheld the decision of the lower court. In so doing, it limited its discussion largely to what it conceived "to be the pivotal issue . . . the constitutionality of the statute requiring daily readings from the Holy Bible."]

CALDWELL, J.

The plaintiffs lean heavily upon the Everson, McCollum, McGowan and Torcaso cases for support and make much of the fact that in those cases, the court, defining the "establishment" clause, used this language: "Neither a state nor the Federal Government can set up a church. Neither can pass laws which aid one religion, aid all religions, or prefer one religion over another. Neither can force or influence a person to go to or remain away from church against his will or force him to profess a belief or disbelief in any religion. . . . In the words of Jefferson the clause against establishment of religion by law was intended to erect 'a wall of separation between Church and State.'"

We are not impressed with the language quoted as being definitive of the "establishment" clause. It goes far beyond the purpose and intent of the authors and beyond any reasonable application to the practical facts of every day life in this country. We feel that the broad language quoted must, in the course of time, be further receded from, if weight is to be accorded the true purpose of the First Amendment. . .

.   .   .   .

The concept of God has been and is so interwoven into every aspect of American institutions that to attack this concept is to threaten the very fiber of our existence as a nation. . . .

.   .   .   .

It is beyond the realm of possibility for this court to reconcile our conception of the First Amendment with the too broad language of the several decisions relied upon by the plaintiff. Nor have we been able to reconcile the several retreats, modifications and hair-splitting distinctions written in those opinions and made to accommodate varying statements of facts. . . .

. . . .

We think it necessary that, unless otherwise clearly commanded by the plain language of the statutes or the Constitution, the courts refrain from purely philosophical invasions of the Constitution or long established and accepted customs of the vast majority of the American people. The recurrent whittling away of the bedrock foundations of our society can be nothing short of destructive of free government. Every doubtful judicial withdrawal of the sovereignty of the states or the traditional freedoms of the people weakens the fabric of the nation and the confidence of its citizens. If the Constitution be wrong it should be corrected by amendment and not judicial usurpation.

. . . .

In principle there is no substantial difference between the excusing of the Zorach students who wished to attend religious exercises elsewhere and the excusing of the Dade County students who do not wish to hear the Bible read in school. And, in substance, there is no difference in principle between the three and five minutes' use of Dade County public school facilities for the reading of the Bible to those who wish to hear it and the non-use, during school hours, of such facilities in Zorach while those who wish religious instruction elsewhere are excused from the premises. To beg the question between the facts in Zorach and the instant case is to engage in cynical trivialities.

It does not appear by the pleadings and testimony that there is any serious contention that the children of the plaintiffs have suffered or will suffer any measurable psychological trauma as a consequence of the reading of the Bible, either in or out of their presence. Rather, it seems that this is just another case in which the tender sensibilities of certain minorities are sought to be protected against the allegedly harsh laws and customs enacted and established by the more rugged pioneers of the Nation. . . .

. . . .

We are sensible of the extent to which the sophistries of agnosticism have gained credence. And we acknowledge the trend toward the preference of minorities over the majority and toward the requiring of the majority, which seem never to suffer psychological trauma, to yield up its cherished customs and rights. . . .

For all practical purposes there are now in the world just two forms of government, loosely denominated Democracy and Communism. The vital difference between the two is that the Democracies accept religion and guarantee its free exercise, in one form or another, as part of the day to day lives of their people, whereas Communism has banished religion, except as it may be bootlegged in the dark and inhospitable corners. . . .

We feel it equally imperative that we preserve the safeguards of the Constitution against all violations of the "establishment" and "free exercise" clauses and, at the same time, preserve those clauses and the rights of the States and the people thereunder against weasel-worded constructions and distinctions designed to impute to them either more or less than was originally intended. But typical of the American custom of meeting the other side more than halfway, is the paradox of the appellee school board insuring the free exercise of religion while, by mandatory statute, it must teach the history, doctrines, objectives and techniques of Communism. Thus the school board affords the atheists the freedom of hearing or not hearing the Bible read while it requires that all students, without choice, be taught the facts of Communism, the antithesis of the Bible.

.   .   .   .

An examination of the Everson, Zorach and McCollum cases convinces us of the practical impossibility of drawing distinctions between nebulosities. The purpose of the First Amendment was to prevent the abuses prevalent prior to and at the time of its adoption. There is no occasion to strain at gnats in the cause under consideration. There is or there is not a violation of the substantial meaning of the "establishment" clause and the "free exercise" clause. We see no profit in a tweedle-dee, tweedle-dum uncertainty in which the complete and uncompromising separation of church from state is argued but the exception is allowed, nor the sort of indecisiveness thought by Justice Jackson to be best typified by Byron's Julia who "whispering 'I will ne'er consent,'—consented."

Guides for Class Discussion

1. Check the reasoning followed by the court with that employed in *Illinois ex rel. McCollum* v. *Board of Education, infra; Zorach* v. *Clauson, infra;* and *Everson* v. *Board of Education of Township of Ewing, infra.*

2. Compare this decision with that rendered by a federal court in *Schempp* v. *School District of Abington Township, infra.* With which are you in agreement? Give reasons.

3. See *Commonwealth* v. *Renfrew, supra.*

4. What is your reaction to the paradox which the court pointed out, "of the . . . board insuring the free exercise of religion

while, by mandatory statute, it must teach [about] . . . Communism"?

5. How would you describe or characterize the court's philosophy with respect to the interpretation of the constitution?

47. *"A United States District Court . . . has held that compulsory Bible reading is violative of the First Amendment"* (p. 8).

Schempp v. School District of Abington Township,
201 F. Supp. 815 (1962)
(Decided by the United States District Court E. D. Pennsylvania)

[In 1958 plaintiffs brought an action against defendants in this court, the purpose of which was to have a statute that provided for the compulsory reading of ten verses from the Holy Bible at the opening of each school in the state each morning declared unconstitutional. Plaintiffs, who were Unitarians, objected to the statute, primarily, on the ground it violated the First Amendment. The court entered judgment declaring the statute unconstitutional. The defendants appealed to the Supreme Court of the United States, but before the case was decided the legislature amended the law so as to permit any child to be excused from attending Bible reading if his parents so requested. The Supreme Court, recognizing this amendment, vacated the lower court's judgment and remanded the case for such further proceedings as might be appropriate as the result of the amendment. Plaintiffs moved to file a supplemental plea, and the case was retried. The court again held the act unconstitutional. Again the defendants appealed to the United States Supreme Court which, at this writing, has not rendered its decision.]

Biggs, Circuit Judge.

. . . .

It is unnecessary to review the evidence taken at the former hearings or to repeat here the findings of fact set out in our first opinion, reported at D.C. 1959, 177 F. Supp. 398 et seq. The present Bible reading statute permits a student to be excused from attending Bible reading upon the written request of his parent or guardian. The statute itself contains no specific penalty to be imposed upon the teacher who fails to observe its mandate as was the case prior to the 1959 amendment. The teacher, however, who refuses or fails to obey the mandate of the amended statute may have his contract of employment terminated pursuant to 24 P. S. § 11-1122 (Supp. 1960). This is a provision of the Pennsylvania Public School Act which speaks strongly for itself. . . .

.   .   .   .

As to the preliminary questions of law we think we need not say much more than that which is set out under heading "III" of our first opinion, 177 F. Supp. 402-403, except in two respects. The statute now *sub judice* provides, as has been said, that a child may be excused from attendance at the Bible reading on the written request of his parent or guardian. But since, as will appear hereinafter, we decide this controversy on the "Establishment of Religion" clause of the First Amendment the exculpatory phrase cannot aid the defendants' argument that the doctrine of abstention is applicable for, as we will show, there is religious establishment in this case whether pupils are or are not excused from attendance at the morning exercises. . . .

The attendance by the minor plaintiffs, Roger and Donna Schempp, at the Abington Senior High School is compulsory. . . . The reading of ten verses of the Holy Bible under the present statute also is compelled by law. The reading of the verses, even without comment, possesses a devotional and religious character and constitutes in effect a religious observance. The devotional and religious nature of the morning exercises is made all the more apparent by the fact that the Bible reading is followed immediately by a recital in unison by the pupils of the Lord's Prayer. The fact that some pupils, or theoretically all pupils, might be excused from attendance at the exercises does not mitigate the obligatory nature of the ceremony for the "new" Section 1516, as did the statute prior to its 1959 amendment, unequivocally requires the exercises to be held every school day in every school in the Commonwealth. The exercises are held in the school buildings and perforce are conducted by and under the authority of the local school authorities and during school sessions. Since the statute requires the reading of the "Holy Bible", a Christian document, the practice, as we said in our first opinion, prefers the Christian religion. The record demonstrates that it was the intention of the General Assembly of the Commonwealth of Pennsylvania to introduce a religious ceremony into the public schools of the Commonwealth.

.   .   .   .

We hold the statute as amended unconstitutional on the ground that it violates the "Establishment of Religion" clause of the First Amend-

ent made applicable to the Commonwealth of Pennsylvania by the
urteenth Amendment. We find it unnecessary to pass upon any other
ntention made by the plaintiffs in respect to the unconstitutionality of
e statute or of the practices thereunder.

Guides for Class Discussion

1. Compare this case with *McCollum* v. *Board of Education, infra*.
2. Compare this case with *Zorach* v. *Clauson, infra*.
3. See *Commonwealth* v. *Renfrew, supra*.
4. It is frequently argued that the courts, in protecting the rights of minority groups, as in this case, fail to consider the wishes of the majority. How would you answer this?

8. "*A board rule that permits religious instructors to come into public-school building to give sectarian instruction to pupils hose parents desire it violates the federal constitution*" (p. 8).

LLINOIS EX REL. McCOLLUM v. BOARD OF EDUCATION,
333 U. S. 203 (1948)
(Decided by the Supreme Court of the United States)

[This case was brought to test the constitutionality of a released-
ime program being carried on by the Champaign, Illinois, public
chools. On a certain day each week children, whose parents
ranted them permission so to do, were excused from their regular
chool work to attend classes of their choice in religious education.
These classes, taught by teachers supplied by the Council on
Religious Education, were held in the public school buildings.
Pupils whose parents did not desire them to attend such classes
vere required to remain in school and spend their time on their
chool work. The mother of a child in attendance brought this
action for a writ of mandamus to compel the board to cease
permitting the holding of such classes in the schools during school
ours on the ground that such action was violative of the First

Amendment. The state's highest court dismissed her petition and she appealed to the Supreme Court of the United States which reversed the state court and ruled in her favor. The decision was rendered by a divided court.]

MR. JUSTICE BLACK delivered the opinion of the Court.

This case relates to the power of the state to utilize its tax-supported public school system in aid of religious instruction insofar as that power may be restricted by the First and Fourteenth Amendments to the Federal Constitution.

. . . .

Appellant's petition for mandamus alleged that religious teachers, employed by private religious groups, were permitted to come weekly into the school buildings during the regular hours set apart for secular teaching, and then and there for a period of thirty minutes substitute their religious teaching for the secular education provided under the compulsory education law. The petitioner charged that this joint public-school religious-group program violated the First and Fourteenth Amendments to the United States Constitution. The prayer of her petition was that the Board of Education be ordered to "adopt and enforce rules and regulations prohibiting all instruction in and teaching of religious education in all public schools in Champaign School District Number 71. . . and in all public school houses and buildings in said district when occupied by public schools."

. . . .

The foregoing facts. . . show the use of tax-supported property for religious instruction and the close cooperation between the school authorities and the religious council in promoting religious education. . . . This is beyond all question a utilization of the tax-established and tax-supported public school system to aid religious groups to spread their faith. And it falls squarely under the ban of the First Amendment (made applicable to the States by the Fourteenth) as we interpreted it in *Everson* v. *Board of Education*, 330 U.S. 1. . . .

. . . .

Here not only are the State's tax-supported public school buildings used for the dissemination of religious doctrines. The State also affords sectarian groups an invaluable aid in that it helps to provide pupils for the religious classes through use of the State's compulsory public school machinery. This is not separation of Church and State.

The cause is reversed and remanded to the State Supreme Court for proceedings not inconsistent with this opinion.

Reversed and Remanded

Guides for Class Discussion

1. What does the "wall of separation" between church and state actually separate?
2. Does this decision have the effect of declaring all released-time programs unconstitutional? Explain.
3. On what basis did the court arrive at its decision?

9. "A school board may . . . permit pupils to be released from *chool time to attend sectarian instruction [outside school build-*gs]" (p. 8).

ZORACH V. CLAUSON,
343 U. S. 306 (1952)
(Decided by the Supreme Court of the United States)

[Four years after rendering its decision in the *McCollum* case, *upra*, the Supreme Court gave judicial approval to a "released-*me*" program in New York. This program, while quite similar the Champaign, Illinois, program, differed from it in at least ne major respect—it was conducted off of school property, rather *han* on it. This decision was rendered by a divided court.]

MR. JUSTICE DOUGLAS delivered the opinion of the Court.

.   .   .   .

It takes obtuse reasoning to inject any issue of the "free exercise" of *eligion* into the present case. No one is forced to go to the religious *lassroom* and no religious exercise or instruction is brought to the class-*ooms* of the public schools. A student need not take religious instruc-*ion*. He is left to his own desires as to the manner or time of his re-_gious_ devotions, if any.

.   .   .   .

We would have to press the concept of separation of Church and *tate* to . . . extremes to condemn the present law on constitutional *rounds*. The nullification of this law would have wide and profound *ffects*. A Catholic student applies to his teachers for permission to leave *he* school during hours on a Holy Day of Obligation to attend a mass.

A Jewish student asks his teacher for permission to be excused for Yom Kippur. A Protestant wants the afternoon off for a family baptismal ceremony. In each case the teacher requires parental consent in writing. In each case the teacher, in order to make sure the student is not a truant, goes further and requires a report from the priest, the rabbi, or the minister. The teacher in other words cooperates in a religious program to the extent of making it possible for her students to participate in it. Whether she does it occasionally for a few students, regularly for one, or pursuant to a systematized program designed to further the religious needs of all the students does not alter the character of the act.

We are a religious people whose institutions presuppose a Supreme Being. . . . When the state encourages religious instruction or cooperates with religious authorities by adjusting the schedule of public events to sectarian needs, it follows the best of our traditions. For it then respects the religious nature of our people and accommodates the public service to their spiritual needs. To hold that it may not would be to find in the Constitution a requirement that the government show a callous indifference to religious groups. That would be preferring those who believe in no religion over those who do believe. Government may not finance religious groups nor undertake religious instruction nor blend secular and sectarian education nor use secular institutions to force one or some religion on any person. But we find no constitutional requirement which makes it necessary for government to be hostile to religion and to throw its weight against efforts to widen the effective scope of religious influence. The government must be neutral when it comes to competition between sects. . . . But it can close its doors or suspend its operations as to those who want to repair to their religious sanctuary for worship or instruction. No more than that is undertaken here.

· · · · · · · · · · · ·

In the *McCollum* case the classrooms were used for religious instruction and the force of the public school was used to promote that instruction. Here, as we have said, the public schools do no more than accommodate their schedules to a program of outside religious instruction. We follow the *McCollum* case. But we cannot expand it to cover the present released time program unless separation of Church and State means that public institutions can make no adjustments of their schedules to accommodate the religious needs of the people. We cannot read into the Bill of Rights such a philosophy of hostility to religion.

Affirmed

Guides for Class Discussion

1. What does this decision add to the knowledge of the wall that separates church and state that was not previously expressed in the *McCollum* case?

2. Is the opinion of the court entirely consistent with its opinion in the *McCollum* case?
3. As a result of the decisions in the *McCollum* and *Zorach* cases, What is the law relating to released time?

0. "It is not violative of the federal constitution for a school oard to pay the cost of transportation of pupils to a parochial chool" (p. 8).

EVERSON V. BOARD OF EDUCATION OF THE
TOWNSHIP OF EWING,
330 U.S. 1 (1947)
(Decided by the Supreme Court of the United States)

[The federal constitution guarantees certain rights to the individual. The First Amendment says: "Congress shall make no law respecting an establishment of religion, or prohibiting the free exercise thereof." The Supreme Court, following the adoption of the Fourteenth Amendment, held that a clause found therein which provided that "no state shall make or enforce any law which shall abridge the privileges and immunities of citizens of the United States," had the effect of making the First Amendment applicable to the states as well as the federal government.

[This case grew out of the actions of a school board in reimbursing parents of parochial-school pupils for money spent in sending their children to school on buses of a local transportation system. By statute, the board was authorized to permit pupils attending any school "other than a public school, except such school as is operated for profit in whole or in part" to ride on school busses. It also provided that the board "may make rules and contracts for the transportation" of children who live at a remote distance from the schoolhouse, including those in attendance at nonprofit, nonpublic schools. Acting under this statute, a school board reimbursed parents of pupils in attendance at Catholic parochial schools. The order of the board specifically designated such schools. A taxpayer then brought this action against the board challenging its right so to do. The state court ruled in favor of the board and the taxpayer appealed. He insisted that the statute and the board's actions under it were violative of either the state or the federal constitution. The court, in arriving at its decision, which was not unanimous, considered the First and Fourteenth Amendments.]

MR. JUSTICE BLACK delivered the opinion of the Court.

.   .   .   .

The only contention here is that the state statute and the resolution, insofar as they authorized reimbursement to parents of children attending parochial schools, violates the Federal Constitution in these two respects, which to some extent overlap. *First.* They authorize the State to take by taxation the private property of some and bestow it upon others, to be used for their own private purposes. This, it is alleged, violates the due process clause of the Fourteenth Amendment. *Second.* The statute and the resolution forced inhabitants to pay taxes to help support and maintain schools which are dedicated to, and which regularly teach, the Catholic Faith. This is alleged to be a use of state power to support church schools contrary to the prohibition of the First Amendment which the Fourteenth Amendment made applicable to the states.

.   .   .   .

It is much too late to argue that legislation intended to facilitate the opportunity of children to get a secular education serves no public purpose. . . .

.   .   .   .

Measured by these standards, we cannot say that the First Amendment prohibits New Jersey from spending tax-raised funds to pay the bus fares of parochial school pupils as a part of a general program under which it pays the fares of pupils attending public and other schools. It is undoubtedly true that children are helped to get to church schools. There is even a possibility that some of the children might not be sent to the church schools if the parents were compelled to pay their children's bus fares out of their own pockets when transportation to a public school would have been paid for by the State. The same possibility exists where the state requires a local transit company to provide reduced fares to school children including those attending parochial schools, or where a municipally owned transportation system undertakes to carry all school children free of charge. Moreover, state-paid policemen, detailed to protect children going to and from church schools from the very real hazards of traffic, would serve much the me purpose and accomplish much the same result as state provisions tended to guarantee free transportation of a kind which the state ems to be best for the school children's welfare. . . . Of course, cutting f church schools from these services, so separate and so indisputably arked off from the religious function, would make it far more difficult for the schools to operate. But such is obviously not the purpose the First Amendment. That Amendment requires the state to be a utral in its relations with groups of religious believers and non-believers; it does not require the state to be their adversary. State power no more to be used so as to handicap religions than it is to favor em.

. . . .

The First Amendment has erected a wall between church and state. hat wall must be kept high and impregnable. We could not approve e slightest breach. New Jersey has not breached it here.

Guides for Class Discussion

1. Does this case sanction the use of public funds for religious purposes?
2. In light of the board rule authorizing reimbursement where children attended "Catholic parochial schools" would you agree that discrimination against pupils attending other than Catholic nonprofit schools was a major issue?
4. What are some implication of this decision?
5. Compare this case with *Illinois ex rel. McCollum* v. *Board of Education, supra;* with *Zorach* v. *Clauson, supra.*

51. ". . . *a board of education may expel from school any pupi*
who disobeys any reasonable rule of the board" (p. 9).

McLean Independent School District v. Andrews,
333 S.W. (2d) 886 (Tex.) (1960)
(Decided by the Court of Civil Appeals of Texas. Amarillo)

[This case came to the higher court on an appeal by the distric
from a decision of the lower court permanently enjoining it "from
expelling or suspending Marsha Andrews . . . for past or future
violations" of a board rule which required that pupils drivin
automobiles to school must park them on the parking lot and no
move them until 3:45 P.M., except by special permission. The gir
in question drove an automobile to school but parked it at a privat
residence one block north of the high school, drove it home fo
lunch each day, then drove back, and parked it in the same plac
until school was out. The lower court found that the girl violate
the rule but that it was void because the board did not have th
power or authority to enact it. The higher court reversed the lowe
court.]

Chapman, Justice.

. . . .

The courts of Texas have consistently upheld the actions of schoo
authorities in promulgating rules to insure proper conduct and decorur
of the students designed for the good of the schools as a whole whe
such rules have not shown a clear abuse of power and discretion or
violation of law. So let us look at the facts.

The uncontroverted testimony given in this case by the President c
the McLean Board of Trustees shows that before the rule in questio
was passed 50 to 60 automobiles driven to school by the children woul
be driven away at the noon hour. The record shows the high schoo
its grounds and parking areas, and the grade school and playgrounc
were all located in the same immediate vicinity . . .; that small chi
dren would be there at the time the cars were leaving; that befor
passing the regulation "it got to be quite a traffic problem, a hazar
and our sole thought in passing this rule was for the protection of 35
or 60 children that we have in school. We didn't pick out any on
person, we weren't trying to make a hardship case on anybody. Ou
only thought was for the benefit of our children in the McLean school
That is the reason we passed the rule. Anybody I think that could b

here at the time these 50 or 60 cars were trying to leave that parking
ot and go to lunch could see the problem we had."

.   .   .   .

The high school principal testified he talked to Marsha on several
occasions and warned her that she would have to be suspended if she
did not comply with the rule in question. The testimony shows the
following conversation between them: ". . . there is no reason in the
world why you shouldn't drive it in the parking lot." She said, "I don't
think my daddy wants me to do that."

The Superintendent of Schools testified:

"The traffic of the students leaving the school after having a joy ride
around the school, up the streets and throughout the city of McLean,
and also riding on the highways; that has been their big problem, and
we are faced with it every year. It wasn't something we just thought
up overnight. It was a problem that has been discussed every year, to
my knowledge, since I have been in McLean."

.   .   .   .

"We have had cars run together, and the time when I was high school
principal we had a little boy run over in front of the elementary school."
He further testified in effect that the problem had become more
acute each year by reason of the economy of the area, making it possible for more students to have cars to drive to school and that since
the rule was invoked conditions had been a hundred per cent better.

.   .   .   .

. . . we are forced to the conclusion that the learned trial judge was
in error in holding that the Board of Trustees of the McLean Independent School District exceeded its authority in promulgating the rule
in question. The regulation was not for the purpose of exercising authority over the use of public streets and highways at all (as suggested
by the appellees' reply point) but for the purpose of controlling the
conduct of the students to the end that student pedestrians on the
streets adjacent to the schools might be safe from student operated
automobiles and that better order, decorum and discipline might pre-
vail at the noon recess. We do not believe they abused their discretion in so doing.

.   .   .   .

The judgment of the trial court is reversed and rendered that the
appellant did not exceed its authority in promulgating the rule in question and suspending Marsha Andrews for its violation after repeated
warnings.

Guides for Class Discussion

1. What test did the court apply to the rule in question?
2. How do you think the court would have ruled had the board forbidden students to drive to school?
3. How do you think it would have ruled had the board also required the pupils to pay a parking fee?

52. ". . . *a pupil may be expelled for general misconduct that does not violate any specific rule of the board*" (p. 9).

STATE v. DISTRICT BOARD,
135 Wis. 619, 116 N.W. 232 (1908)
(Decided by the Supreme Court of Wisconsin)

[This was an action in mandamus to require a district board of school directors to reinstate relator's children who had been suspended from the high school. The children in question took a poem written by a member of the senior class, which was a "take-off on the rules of the school," to the publisher of a weekly newspaper and requested him to print it in the paper. This the publisher did. As a result the children were suspended until such time as they agreed to apologize. The parent contended that the children had committed only a harmless act, one that took place after school had closed and outside of the school building, where the children were under the control of the principal. The defendants contended that the publication of the poem was detrimental to the interests of the school, and it tended to hold up the school, its discipline, and its teachers to public contempt and ridicule and tended to develop an attitude of hostility toward the teachers on the part of the pupils. The lower court ruled in favor of the school board and the higher court upheld the decision of the lower court.]

BASHFORD, J. . . .

. . . .

The remaining assignments of error relate to the power of the school authorities to suspend the offending pupils for the misconduct, which was established by the undisputed evidence. The authority to suspend the pupils from the privileges of the school is denied by the appellant, unless the offense was a violation of some rule prescribed by the board, or involved moral turpitude, or was committed during school hours in the schoolroom, or in the presence of the master and other pupils. . . . But, it is urged that in the instant case no rule had been prescribed by the board or by the teacher relating to the misconduct complained of. . . .

. . . We have been referred to no decision directly holding that the school authorities can suspend a pupil for misconduct after school hours, unless the offense is a violation of established rules, or is committed in the schoolhouse or upon the school grounds, or in the presence of the master and other pupils. There is abundant authority, however, that the school board or the teacher may make rules to govern the conduct of the pupils after school hours, and punish a violation thereof by suspension from attendance upon school. . . .

It is clear, therefore, that a rule might have been adopted by the school authorities to meet the situation here presented. This court. . . recognizes certain obligations on the part of the pupil, which are inherent in any proper school system, and which constitute the common law of the school, and which may be enforced without the adoption in advance of any rules upon the subject. This court therefore holds that the school authorities have the power to suspend a pupil for an offense committed outside of school hours, and not in the presence of the teacher which has a direct and immediate tendency to influence the conduct of other pupils while in the schoolroom, to set at naught the proper discipline of the school, to impair the authority of the teachers, and to bring them into ridicule and contempt. Such power is essential to the preservation of order, decency, decorum, and good government in the public schools.

. . . The trial court has found that the act complained of does not evince an abuse of discretion on the part of the teachers, but rather an earnest desire to counsel, admonish, and discipline the pupils for their own good as well as for the good of the school. That conclusion is supported by the testimony and is here approved. This court is not called upon to decide as to the wisdom of the action of the school authorities, but only as to their jurisdiction within proper limits.

The judgment of the court below is affirmed.

Guides for Class Discussion

1. See *McLean Independent School District* v. *Andrews, supra.*
2. Are you in agreement with the court's reasoning? Give reasons.

53. *"In the nature of his duties, a teacher has the right to exclude a pupil from school until the matter has been passed upon by the school board"* (p. 9).

STATE v. BURTON,
45 Wis. 150 (1878)
(Decided by the Supreme Court of Wisconsin)

[When the high-school principal at Janesville, Wisconsin, suspended and expelled a 16-year-old boy from school, his father asked to have him readmitted; but the principal refused to comply with the demand, whereupon this action was brought to compel the boy's readmission. The defendant admitted he suspended the boy from the privileges of the school for continued misconduct after his teachers had advised and counseled with him. The principal stated that he immediately reported his actions in writing to the board of education and informed it regarding the character and date of the offenses for which suspension was made, and that he also notified the boy's father. The principal stated that when the boy manifested and expressed regret for his misconduct and gave "a sincere promise of future good-conduct" he would be readmitted as a pupil. The lower court supported the parent, and the principal appealed to the higher court, which reversed the lower court and remanded the cause for further proceedings according to the law.]

LYON, J. . . .

On the argument of the appeal, counsel informed us that the learned circuit judge held that the defendant has no power to suspend a pupil for any cause, such power being vested by law exclusively in the board of education, and that the demurrer to the return was sustained on that ground. Whether the defendant has such power of suspension, and, if so, whether it was properly exercised in the present case, are the controlling questions to be determined on this appeal.

While the principal or teacher in charge of a public school is subordinate to the school board or board of education of his district or city, and must enforce rules and regulations adopted by the board for the government of the school, and execute all its lawful orders in that behalf, he does not derive all his power and authority in the school and over his pupils from the affirmative action of the board. He stands for the time being *in loco parentis* to his pupils, and because of that rela ion he must necessarily exercise authority over them in many things concerning which the board may have remained silent. . . .

The teacher is responsible for the discipline of his school, and for the progress, conduct and deportment of his pupils. It is his imperative duty to maintain good order, and to require of his pupils a faithful performance of their duties. If he fails to do so, he is unfit for his position. To enable him to discharge these duties effectually, he must necessarily have the power to enforce prompt obedience to his lawful commands. For this reason the law gives him the power, in proper cases, to inflict corporal punishment upon refractory pupils. But there are cases of misconduct for which such punishment is an inadequate remedy. If the offender is incorrigible, suspension or expulsion is the only adequate remedy. In general, no doubt, the teacher should report a case of that kind to the proper board for its action in the first instance, if no delay will necessarily result from that course prejudicial to the best interests of the school. But the conduct of the recusant pupil may be such that his presence in the school for a day or an hour may be disastrous to the discipline of the school, and even to the morals of the other pupils. In such a case, it seems absolutely essential to the welfare of the school that the teacher should have the power to suspend the offender at once from the privileges of the school; and he must necessarily decide for himself whether the case requires that remedy.

Guides for Class Discussion

1. See *State* v. *District Board, supra;* and *McLean Independent School District* v. *Andrews, supra.*
2. Do you think that the rule laid down is equitable to both teachers and pupils? Give reasons.
3. In light of what the court said, what is the general rule regarding suspension or expulsion of pupils?

54. *"Unless the statute requires it, it is not necessary to give the pupil notice of his suspension or a hearing before excluding him from school"* (p. 9).

FLORY V. SMITH,
145 Va. 164, 134 S.E. 360 (1926)
(Decided by the Supreme Court of Appeals of Virginia)

[In this case a school board enacted a rule forbidding children to leave the campus between the hours of 9:30 A.M. and 3:35 P.M. unless they were accompanied by a teacher. Parents of two children asked to have their children relieved of this restriction and be permitted to eat their midday meal at home, situated about a mile from the school, or to eat it with their father at a hotel in the town. This privilege was denied by the principal, and the children, in spite of the denial and in violation of the rule, took their midday meal with their father at the hotel. This they continued to do when, because of the infraction of the rule, they were suspended from school. The parents then filed this action contesting the validity of the rule, on the ground that it was an unreasonable regulation in restraint of the liberty of themselves and their children. The school board demurred and the lower court overruled the demurrer and entered a decree restraining the principal from prohibiting the children from leaving the school grounds at noon. On appeal, the higher court reversed the decision of the lower court. Among other things, the parents in this case contended that they had been penalized without notice. In its decision the court held that the fact the parents were notified of the suspension was all the notice required to legalize the action taken.]

CAMPBELL, J. . . .

. . . .

The last contention of appellees is that they have been penalized without notice and deprived of their right to seek redress by appeal. Section 659 of the Code makes it the duty of the district school board (now the county school board) to explain, enforce, and observe the school laws, and to make rules for the government of the school. It is further provided in this section that the authority thus given shall be subject to review by the board of appeal provided by section 632 of

he Code. This latter section provides how the school trustee electoral
board shall hear any such appeal.

By express enactment, the act of 1922, the county school board,
created by this act, is "vested with all the powers and charged with
all the duties and obligations hitherto vested in, or conferred or imposed
upon, the several district school boards."

Section 961 of the Code provides, among other things, that a teacher
of a public free school may, for a sufficient cause, suspend pupils from
attendance on the school until the case is decided by the board of school
trustees; and it is further provided that, in all such cases of suspension
the teacher shall report the facts to the board and to the parent or
guardian of the child suspended. Immediately upon the suspension of
appellees' child, notice of such suspension was given to the father, We
are of the opinion that this was sufficient notice; that upon the receipt
thereof he had the absolute right to have the matter reviewed by the
county school board within a reasonable time from the date of the
receipt of such notice.

For the reasons stated, the decree of the circuit court must be reversed, and this court will enter a decree dismissing the bill of complaint.

Reversed.

Guides for Class Discussion

1. Do you think the rule in question was reasonable? Give reasons.
2. Are you in agreement with the court that pupils need not be
   given notice and a hearing before expelling them, or do you
   think they should be given such notice and a hearing? Give
   reasons.

55. " *A board of education does not have authority to expel a pupil from school for an indefinite period . . .*" (p. 9).

BOARD OF EDUCATION v. HELSTON,
32 Ill. App. 300 (1889)
(Decided by the Appellate Court of Illinois)

[When a boy was suspended from school for refusing to divulge to the superintendent the name of another pupil whom he thought was guilty of defacing school property, his father brought this action in mandamus to compel the board to restore the boy to his privileges as a pupil. It appears that the board suspended the boy in November, 1888. In February, 1889, he appeared before the board and still persisted in his refusal to divulge any information. He was requested to ask his mother to come with him so that the board might confer with her upon the matter, whereupon he applied "the most profane and obscene epithets to the board and went away." The lower court held in favor of the pupil and the higher court reversed the lower court.]

WALL, J. . . .

. . . .

It appears from the record that the relator was suspended from the school November 9, 1888, until he would comply with the requirements of the board. This suspension would not be construed to continue beyond the school year then current, and as that year has now expired the relator presumably is not now debarred of school privileges. The only point having legal significance remaining in the record is as to the costs in the court below which were adjudged against the board. To determine the propriety of that judgment it will be necessary to consider the facts presented by the pleadings.

. . . .

So here every pupil, when called upon by the superintendent or by the board, should, as a matter of duty and loyalty to what is essential for the common welfare, freely state anything within his knowledge not self-criminating, that will assist in bringing the offender to justice and thereby tend to the repression of all such offenses.

If he refuses to do this he is guilty of disobedience, for which reasonable punishment may be inflicted. By the provisions of the school law,

Secs. 49, 83, the board may suspend or expel a pupil for "gross disobedience or misconduct."

.   .   .   .

In this case, upon the facts disclosed by the answer, the board was
clearly warranted in suspending the relator. He was guilty of gross disobedience in refusing to furnish what information he had when called
on for that purpose. For such refusal of a witness to testify before a
grand jury or upon a trial he may be fined and imprisoned.

By his misconduct, when before the board in February, the relator
forfeited all rights to reinstatement until suitable reparation therefor
was tendered.

It would be unwise and unreasonable to open the door of the court
to one so forgetful of duty and so wanting in the respect due from a
youth to his superiors in age and authority. Here is a boy of fourteen
who has defied the proper command of his school superintendent and
who has been guilty of an outrageous breach of decorum toward the
board, who were for the time being his judges, asking the law to reinstate him as a pupil. If he could succeed under those circumstances,
the power of the superintendent and the board would justly be regarded
as very insignificant and the influence of the example would be ex-
ceedingly unfortunate.

Guides for Class Discussion

1. Does this case add anything to your knowledge of the authority of the board to dismiss a pupil for misbehavior?
2. See *State* v. *District Board, supra;* and *McLean Independent
School District* v. *Andrews, supra.*

56. " *If a pupil has been illegally excluded from school he may
obtain a writ of mandamus to enforce his reinstatement*" (p. 9).

Holman v. School Trustees,
77 Mich. 605, 43 N.W. 996 (1889)
(Decided by the Supreme Court of Michigan)

[This was a hearing on an order to show cause why the son of
the plaintiff should not be reinstated in school, from which he had
been suspended. The pupil in question had been suspended because of breaking a window, and his father refused to pay for it.

The father applied to the teacher and requested her to reinstate the boy but she refused, whereupon he asked the trustees to do the same; but they also refused. The father then brought this action for a writ of mandamus to compel the boy's reinstatement. The lower court granted the writ, on the ground the pupil had been illegally excluded. The higher court then affirmed the decision of the lower court.]

Morse, J. . . .

. . . .

. . . But, before he can be thus dealt with, he must be guilty of some willful or malicious act of detriment to the school, and the misconduct must be gross,—something more than a petty or trivial offense against the rules,—or he must be persistent in his disobedience of the proper and reasonable rules and regulations of the school. A boy 10 years old, or even older, cannot be expelled or suspended for a careless act, no matter how negligent, if it is not willful or malicious. The action taken in this case might, to a poor boy, mean indefinite suspension. This rule might in a great many cases, if enforced, prevent the further attendance of pupils at the public schools, while we have laws upon our statute books compelling such attendance. It is not desirable nor permissible that a child may be excluded from the common schools because, by a careless or negligent act, without malice or willfulness, it has injured or damaged school property to such an extent that it is beyond its power, or that of its parent or guardian, to make compensation for it. This would be the effect of the rule, if carried out in many cases. In the present case, no doubt, the father could have replaced this glass without serious financial detriment, and it would have been much cheaper for him to have done so. But he saw fit to stand upon his rights, as he was privileged to do, and by so doing test the power and authority of school boards in this state to adopt and enforce such rules as the one before us, which, in other instances, might deprive poor children who are careless, as all children are careless, of the right to a common-school education, which the laws and policy of our state have guaranteed to them so carefully that the parent is punished if he neglects or refuses to give his children the benefit of the public schools. The writ will issue as prayed.

Guides for Class Discussion

1. Compare the decision in this case with *McLean Independent School District* v. *Andrews, supra;* and *State* v. *District Board, supra.*

2. In case a child is illegally excluded, does the parent have any other remedy than a writ of mandamus?
3. Do you agree with the court's reasoning to the effect that a parent cannot be compelled to pay for school property damaged by his child? Give reasons.

57. *"Under the common law the teacher stands in loco parentis . . . to . . . his pupils [and] . . . may . . . administer any reasonable corporal punishment for offences within the jurisdiction of the board of education . . . [with immunity] if he acts without malice, and inflicts no lasting or permanent injury upon the pupil [so it is generally held]" (p. 9).*

STATE V. LUTZ,
113 N.E. (2d) 757 (Ohio) (1953)
(Decided by the Court of Common Pleas of Ohio, Stark County)

[A teacher who paddled a boy for throwing a stone at a little girl while on the way to school "and then fibbed about it" was convicted of assault and battery before a Municipal Judge. From this conviction the teacher appealed. The paddle used was of normal proportions, and the teacher struck the boy from six to fifteen times. His buttocks became vividly discolored, but cleared up in about five days although some tenderness remained. It appears that the boy was an epileptic and had three seizures following the spanking.]

McLAUGHLIN, Judge

. . . .

This case does not present any new, unusual or novel questions of law. Like situations have confronted our courts since schools have existed. Every text book of law contains clear and understandable statements that have application here. Nearly every State has its leading cases on the subject of corporal punishment of a pupil by a teacher. Ohio is no exception.

When a teacher gives a pupil corporal punishment and is charged criminally therefor, certain fundamental proposition [*sic*] of law come to mind.

First, the teacher stands in loco parentis (i.e., in the place of a parent), and acts in a quasi judicial capacity and is not liable for an error in judgment in the matter of punishment.

Second, the teacher's responsibility attaches home to home (i.e., while the pupil is on the way to and from school).

Third, there is a presumption of correctness of the teacher's actions.

Fourth, there is a presumption that the teacher acts in good faith.

Fifth, mere, excessive or severe punishment on the part of the teacher does not constitute a crime unless it is of such a nature as to produce or threaten lasting or permanent injury, or unless the State has shown that it was administered with either express malice (i.e., spite, hatred or revenge), or implied malice (i.e., a wrongful act wantonly done without just cause or excuse), and beyond a reasonable doubt.

Sixth, the defendant teacher is entitled to all the benefits and safeguards of the well-known presumption of innocence.

.   .   .   .

. . . We find on Page 6 of . . . [the trial court's] written opinion and finding these words, "This evidence as well as the remainder of the evidence in this case shocks the sensibilities of this Court as this Court believes it would shock the sensibilities of the average individual under these circumstances, regardless of whether or not he is a disciplinarian of the old school."

. . . "Was the punishment in the case at Bar so severe, so excessive and so cruel as to be shocking to every right thinking man?" If so, then it was "punishment far in excess of what the law authorizes one standing in loco parentis to inflict," and malice will be implied.

This Court has examined the photographic exhibit of the boy's buttocks, and has carefully perused the record as to all bits of evidence concerning the severity of this paddling, and after weighing the evidence we find nothing that shocks the sensibilities of this Court or points to any fact of excessive severity or cruelty. School day memories of the average individual, including this Court, will recall many experiences of corporal punishment more severe than this one properly given and of great benefit to the pupil and the school.

This corporal punishment came to the attention of a number of individuals without shocking their sensibilities.

.   .   .   .

Next, what does the record show as to any production or threatened production of lasting or permanent injuries. The boy was examined by his family physician on the day following the paddling, and the record discloses that the doctor found the vivid discoloring of the boy's buttocks, black and blue, but nowhere does the record disclose that the injuries were such as to require any medical treatment. This boy had been an epileptic since infancy, and his mother did testify that after the paddling he had three such fits, but the record discloses no medical testimony indicating any causal connection between the paddling and the subsequent seizures, the only medical testimony thereon being the family doctor's statement (Record, Page 53), on December 18th, "To my knowledge he has been free from seizures this past year."

How then can it be said that there was any substantial evidence of either physical injuries or cruelty indicating punishment in excess of that which the law authorizes one standing in loco parentis to inflict.

. . . .

The verdict and finding of the trial court is contrary to the manifest weight of the evidence as to severity, cruelty and injury. . . . The verdict of the trial court is not supported by the evidence. . . .

. . . .

This record discloses no evidence which would indicate that this teacher was actuated by any malice, express or implied, or of any serious physical injury or of any punishment in excess of that which the law authorizes one standing in loco parentis to inflict. Contrarily, there is ample evidence to indicate that this teacher acted in good faith with proper motives.

Since we are of the opinion that the trial court should have directed a verdict for the defendant at the conclusion of the State's evidence, this Court will enter such an order at this time and acquit the defendant.

Defendant prepare entry.

Guides for Class Discussion

1. Evaluate the general rule laid down by the court.
2. Do you think the rule is sound? Why or why not?
3. Do you think the court would have held as it did had evidence been introduced to connect the epileptic seizures with the spanking?

58. *"[In actions against teachers who have administered corporal punishment, the courts] in determining whether the punishment is reasonable or not, . . . generally hold that it should be adapted to the nature of the offense and the age, sex, and size of the pupil"* (p. 9).

SUITS V. GLOVER,
260 Ala. 449, 71 So. (2d) 49 (1954)
(Decided by the Supreme Court of Alabama)

[This was an action against a teacher to recover damages for assault and battery allegedly committed as the result of administering corporal punishment to a pupil. The pupil was eight and one-half years old, "well developed, fat and in good health." A jury trial in the lower court resulted in a verdict in favor of the teacher, and the plaintiff appealed. The higher court affirmed the decision of the lower court.]

SIMPSON, Justice.

.   .   .   .

There was no conflict but that certain punishment was administered to the appellant, a school pupil, by the appellee, a schoolmaster. The evidence was, however, conflicting as to the type of instrument used to administer the punishment; the appellant's evidence tending to show that he was whipped with a slat from an apple crate and the appellee's evidence tending to show that the instrument used was a ping-pong paddle, commonly used by the school for administering such punishment. There was evidence that the appellee was responsible for maintaining order and discipline and to administer corporal punishment as was deemed necessary as punishment for infractions of the school rules. Furthermore there was evidence of an infraction of the school rules by the appellant, the nature of which was insubordination and scuffling in the school hall. The appellant's medical expert testified that in his opinion there was no permanent injury and the evidence showed that the appellant remained in school the remainder of the school day the incident occurred (February 22nd) and did not miss any time from school, at least until March 9th, except the day following the incident (February 23rd). The evidence further showed that the appellant was eight and a half years old, well developed, fat and in good health; and there was evidence warranting the inference that the appellee was in no wise angry or aggravated with the appellant when he administered the spanking. The evidence was also conflicting on the issue of the severity of the punishment, the appellee's evidence tending to show that the appellant was paddled on his buttocks only, the skin was not broken, and approximately only five licks were administered.

A schoolmaster is regarded as standing in *loco parentis* and has the authority to administer moderate correction to pupils under his care. To be guilty of an assault and battery, the teacher must not only inflict on the child immoderate chastisement, but he must do so with legal malice or wicked motives or he must inflict some permanent injury. In determining the reasonableness of the punishment or the extent of malice, proper matters for consideration are the instrument used and the nature of the offense committed by the child, the age and physical condition of the child, and the other attendant circumstances. . . .

It appears from the foregoing there was evidence which, if believed by the jury, justified the verdict. . . .

Affirmed.

Guides for Class Discussion

1. Compare this case with *State* v. *Lutz, supra*.
2. Does the decision differ from that in *State* v. *Lutz, supra?* Give reasons.

Selected Bibliography

1. Edwards, Newton. *The Courts and the Public Schools*, rev. ed. Chicago: University of Chicago Press, 1955.
2. Garber, Lee O. *Handbook of School Law*. New London, Connecticut: Arthur C. Croft Publications, 1954.
3. Garber, Lee O. *Yearbook of School Law*. "Pupils." Danville, Illinois: The Interstate Printers and Publishers, Inc., annually since 1950.
4. Gauerke, Warren E. *Legal and Ethical Responsibilities of School Personnel*. Englewood Cliffs, New Jersey: Prentice-Hall, Inc., 1959.

5. Hamilton, Robert H. and Paul R. Mort. *The Law and Publ* *Education*, rev. ed. Brooklyn: The Foundation Press, Inc 1959.

6. Kramer, Robert (Ed.). *Law and Contemporary Problem* "School Pupils and the Law." Durham, North Carolina School of Law, Duke University, 1955.

7. Remmlein, Madaline Kinter. *School Law*, rev. ed. Danvill Illinois: The Interstate Printers and Publishers, Inc., 1962.

8. Reutter, E. Edmund, Jr. *Schools and the Law*. ("Leg; Almanac Series," No. 17.) New York: Oceana Publication Inc., 1960.